Henry Peek

Bankruptcy Legislation and Defaulters in the Legal Profession

Henry Peek

Bankruptcy Legislation and Defaulters in the Legal Profession

ISBN/EAN: 9783337123642

Printed in Europe, USA, Canada, Australia, Japan

Cover: Foto ©Suzi / pixelio.de

More available books at **www.hansebooks.com**

BANKRUPTCY LEGISLATION

AND

DEFAULTERS IN THE LEGAL PROFESSION.

PRIZE ESSAYS.

The Prizes Offered by SIR HENRY PEEK, Bart., M.P.

Extract from "The Times," *January*, 1879.

BANKRUPTCY LEGISLATION AND DEFAULTERS IN THE LEGAL PROFESSION.

SIR HENRY PEEK'S PRIZE ESSAY COMPETITION.

NOTICE.

We, the undersigned Referees, have awarded the First Prize of Thirty Guineas to Mr. Herbert T. Round, LL.B.; the Second Prize of Twenty Guineas to Mr. George Wreford; and the Third Prize of Ten Guineas to Mr. W. H. Hazard. We have also given Certificates of Merit to the following Gentlemen (alphabetical order):—Mr. Walter Mills, Mr. James Rigby Smith, and Mr. James White. The Prize Money has been duly distributed; and at Sir Henry Peek's request, each Certificate of Merit was supplemented with a Cheque for Five Guineas. The proceeds of the sale of the reprint of Newspaper Correspondence has been paid over to the Fund of the Solicitors' Benevolent Association. Unsuccessful Papers (sealed up, with Motto indorsed) will be returned on application to Sir Joseph Causton & Sons, Eastcheap, E.C.

FRANCIS K. MUNTON.
ROBERT EVERETT.

London, 30*th December*, 1878.

CONTENTS.

	PAGE
INTRODUCTION	i.
PRÉCIS	v.

FIRST PRIZE.
    Mr. Herbert T. Round, LL.B., B.A.   5

SECOND PRIZE.
    Mr. George Wreford   25

THIRD PRIZE.
    Mr. William H. Hazard   47

CERTIFICATE OF MERIT.
    Mr. Walter Mills   65

CERTIFICATE OF MERIT.
    Mr. James Rigby Smith   81

CERTIFICATE OF MERIT.
    Mr. James White   95

INTRODUCTION.

On 29th January, 1878, Sir HENRY PEEK asked the Solicitor-General in the House of Commons, "Whether he considered it desirable to append in the *Law List* to the names of solicitors who had become bankrupt, information respecting their bankruptcies; and if he could explain the reason why the names of some solicitors did not appear continuously in the *Law List?*"

The Solicitor-General replied, "That he did not consider it fair to give the proposed information in the *Law List*, as he did not see why the stigma of bankruptcy should attach to a solicitor for the rest of his life more than to other classes. The absence of some solicitors' names from the *Law List* was occasioned by their failure to renew their certificates on or before the 1st January."

This incident gave rise to a discussion in the principal legal journals. One of the correspondents, Mr. F. K. MUNTON, a London solicitor, furnished some statistics of insolvency among members of the profession, the accuracy of which was at first challenged, though subsequently fully confirmed. Sir HENRY PEEK alleged that the result of a careful search through the letter D in the *Law List* showed that more than seven per cent. of the London solicitors under that letter had been declared insolvent, and Sir HENRY'S figures being impugned, Mr. MUNTON checked the statement, and publicly corroborated it.

Various suggestions were, in the course of the correspondence, put forward for remedying the evils arising from the continuance in practice of bankrupt solicitors, and the controversy resulted in the offer, by Sir HENRY PEEK, of Prizes for the three best Essays bearing on the question, with especial reference to the points and remedies adverted to in the correspondence, and embracing also the subject of "Bankruptcy Legislation," so far as it might relate to the question of "defaulters in the legal profession."

In the meantime Mr. MUNTON, as a member of the Incorporated Law Society, gave notice that he would move a resolution on the subject, and ask for the appointment of a Vigilance Committee, and in the Report of the Council read at the Annual Meeting on 4th July, 1878, the matter was thus referred to:—"A discussion, which seems to have had "its origin in some private grievance, was raised in the "House of Commons on a suggestion that solicitors who had "been bankrupt or insolvent should be distinguished by some "mark in the *Law List* or otherwise—a proposal so eminently "impracticable and invidious that the Council did not think

"it worth while to take any action on the subject. A mem-
"ber of the Society intimated to the Council his intention of
"bringing forward a resolution on the subject at the forth-
"coming Annual Meeting. It has been suggested, however,
"that if the subject be deserving of notice at all, it would
"more appropriately form the subject of a paper to be read
"at the Annual Provincial Meeting of the Society."

It appears from the *Law Times* of 13th July, 1878, that Mr. MUNTON considered it very undesirable it should go forth to the world that, although the matter had been mentioned to the Council, they did not consider it deserving of notice, but he acquiesced in the suggestion that the discussion might be conveniently deferred. In adopting this course he was probably influenced by the fact that at that period the Essays on the subject had not been sent in; the 30th September, 1878, having been previously fixed on as the date for their delivery.

The decision of the referees appointed to determine as to the merits of the various Essays submitted in response to Sir HENRY PEEK's invitation, was published on the 30th December, 1878, and the three Prizes were awarded to Mr. H. T. ROUND, Mr. G. WREFORD, and Mr. W. H. HAZARD, respectively. Certificates of Merit were also granted to three other gentlemen, viz.:—Mr. W. MILLS, Mr. J. R. SMITH, and Mr. JAMES WHITE.

The six Essays are published *in extenso* in the following pages, but, for the convenience of readers unable to devote the time requisite for their complete perusal, the following classified *Précis* has been compiled,* embracing the points, arguments, and suggestions of the various essayists, without the unnecessary repetition of matter adverted to by two or more writers.

CLASSIFICATION OF MATTERS TREATED OF IN ESSAYS.

I. The status and regulations of the legal profession.

II. Malpractices of solicitors, apart from insolvency.

III. Insolvency and malpractice on the part of fiduciary agents other than solicitors.

IV. The prevalence of sharp practice in business and professional matters, and the state of public feeling in reference to fraud.

V. The progress of insolvency among solicitors as shown by the statistics, and the causes of failures.

VI. The bearing of the Bankruptcy Law on the question of the insolvency of solicitors.

VII. Proposed remedies for checking the insolvency of solicitors.

---

* The Introduction and Précis were written by Mr. WREFORD, who (in a supplementary competition) obtained the first prize for an Epitome of the Essays.

PRÉCIS.

I.—The Status and Regulations of the Legal Profession.

Regulations were made by Parliament in the reign of George II., for the examination and admission of attorneys, but no self-government existed until the reign of George IV., when a society was formed (1825) to which Royal Charters were granted in 1831 and 1845, under the latter of which the Incorporated Law Society was established in its present constitution. The management of this Society is vested in a president and council, and the members in general meeting have power to make bye-laws, admit, suspend or expel members, and to inflict penalties for breach of those bye-laws. Members rendered incapable of practising as solicitors by any competent Court cease to be members of the Society. For a long time solicitors suffered from a feeling of antipathy on the part of the public, but the larger sympathies of the present age have freed them from all sense of ignominy.   Mr. Mills (p. 67) Mr. Hazard (p. 51) (p. 50) (p. 50)

Solicitors display a want of organisation and self-government, owing partly to the absence of public interest. They stand in a peculiar position, both in regard to the administration of justice and the enjoyment of certain privileges and monopolies. All legal work passes through their hands and they are the depositaries of the pecuniary and personal confidence of the public.   Mr. Round (p. 5) (p. 5) (p. 6)

A competent tribunal for enforcing discipline among solicitors does not exist, and the Courts of Law, to which they are subject, are not suited for enforcing professional etiquette or defining matters of conduct. The argument that insolvent solicitors should not be subjected to exceptional treatment would be reasonable if they were on a par with other classes, but they are not. They are a great public body entrusted by the country with an extensive monopoly by reason of their status and respectability, and the establishment of such a monopoly in favour of duly-qualified individuals is the only way by which the public can be efficiently served and protected.   Mr. Mills (p. 76) (p. 66) (p. 68)

Special privileges and immunities are conferred on solicitors, and they are put in a position for acquiring the trust and confidence of the public in an especial manner.   Mr. Wreford (p. 33)

Mr. WHITE (p. 102)
Mr. HAZARD (pp. 53, 54, & 55)

On the other hand, it is asserted by one writer, that no exceptional privileges are conferred on solicitors, and that they are not pre-eminently trusted in a monetary point of view, the trust being not so much that of money or securities as that involved in the confidential relations with clients, and the question of insolvency does not affect this confidence.

(p. 55)

The social government of the legal profession in England is contrasted with that of notaries in France. The latter possess some admirable features of self-government. All speculations or commercial dealings are prohibited, and the enforcement of rules for regulating the proceedings of notaries is entrusted to Chambers of Discipline, which are armed with most complete powers of supervision over the members of the profession. The Chambers, whose members are elected every three years, exercise limited powers without right of appeal, but the extreme penalties of suspension and removal are vested in the higher authorities, whom the Chambers advise. They also exercise a surveillance of a somewhat inquisitorial and degrading character over the private lives of the members. In America the Courts maintain a peculiar jurisdiction over attorneys, by taking cognizance of "complaints on oath," and striking them off the roll for unprofessional conduct not criminally punishable.

II.—MALPRACTICES OF SOLICITORS APART FROM INSOLVENCY.

Mr. ROUND (p. 8)

Malpractice of solicitors as distinguished from bankruptcy, is different in its nature and demands entirely diverse treatment. Bankruptcy is a definite fact—malpractice is a matter of opinion and highly indefinite; and the question of protecting the public against insolvency on the part of solicitors would, as far as *legislation* is concerned, be injured by being mixed up with that of malpractice. Solicitors are liable, as members of the public, to answer to the proper tribunal for breach of duty or any crime. They are also subject to the summary jurisdiction of the Court, which may punish by way of fine, attachment, or suspension or removal from the roll, for misconduct falling short of an indictable offence. The misconduct of which the Courts take cognizance, may even arise in a transaction in which the solicitor is not acting in his professional capacity, in support of which statement several legal authorities are quoted.

(p. 14)

(p. 15)

(pp. 15 & 16)

vii.

Where a solicitor is convicted of actual fraud before a Court of Justice, exemplary punishment is generally meted out to him. But there are many cases of malpractice on the part of solicitors falling short of actual fraud or misappropriation of moneys with which it is desirable to deal. For instance, the obstacles often thrown in the way of clients endeavouring to obtain money or accounts, the operation of the law as to general lien for costs giving unscrupulous solicitors large opportunities of detaining moneys belonging to clients without actually bringing themselves within reach of the criminal law. The unsatisfactory nature of the present procedure for compelling production of accounts and payment over of moneys is also commented on, and it is suggested that all cases of malpractice should be dealt with by the Incorporated Law Society, which should be empowered to apply to the Court to strike defaulters off the roll. Any aggrieved client also to be allowed to prefer his complaint before the Court personally where the Law Society declines to take action. It is also suggested that restrictions should be placed on the receipt of moneys by solicitors on behalf of clients, and that solicitors should be compelled to account periodically to their clients. More stringent regulations might also advantageously be made with reference to the previous status of any candidate for admission as a solicitor.

Mr. WREFORD (p. 33) (p. 34) (p. 35) (p. 40) (p. 41) (p. 46)

The percentage of misconduct in the legal profession cannot be considered unusually large, but general malpractice on the part of solicitors nevertheless demands severer inquisition than it calls forth at present. The object aimed at should be to bring misconduct more within the reach of justice, and this object could be obtained by increasing the powers of the Incorporated Law Society or its council, and entrusting it with jurisdiction to inflict mild penalties on its own authority in cases which now altogether escape punishment; information from private sources to constitute grounds of action by the society.

Mr. HAZARD (p. 59) (p. 61)

Other evils than insolvency among solicitors, and equally serious, arise from the malpractices of those "who are always "on the verge of insolvency, and who adopt all kinds of tricks "and devices, so embarrassing to those who have to deal with "them." From such practitioners the process of obtaining a client's moneys and securities is tedious and inefficient. A

Mr. MILLS (p. 70)

b

Mr Mills (p. 71)	solicitor detaining money and deeds may be called upon by summons to deliver his bill and accounts, and if he disregard the order may be attached for contempt, but may purge the contempt by delivering the bill, still, however, detaining the property till the bill is taxed. As a solicitor is bound to keep
(p. 71)	his accounts constantly ready for production to his client, a summons to produce them should be returnable the following day, and unless produced on the hearing the solicitor should be required to state probable amount of costs, which amount should
(p. 72)	be paid by the client into Court to abide delivery and taxation of bill. The solicitor should then be ordered to deliver deeds and pay over money instanter, and disobedience should involve not only contempt of Court, but also conversion of the property.
(p. 77)	The Incorporated Law Society should prosecute unauthorised or irregular practitioners, just as the Apothecaries' Society prosecutes unlicensed medical men.
Mr. White (p. 99)	General malpractice is not such conduct as would bring a solicitor as a member of the community within the pale of the law, nor such misconduct as would result in his being struck off the rolls, but such acts or omissions as would be rightly designated "sharp practice," "dishonourable," or "discreditable."
(p. 98)	Failure to take out the annual certificate before the 1st January should not be considered a malpractice, nor as evidence of intentional neglect. A man of defaulting proclivities would be careful to have his name in the *Law List*, as its appearance there is evidence that he is a solicitor, while its absence would cause inconvenience and annoyance. The real causes are care-
(p. 104)	lessness, accident, or impecuniosity. While malpractices, as well as insolvency, exist among solicitors, and require a remedy, they are not more numerous in proportion than those of other professions and callings, and the privileges enjoyed by solicitors are not so great as to give the public a right to expect from
(p. 104)	them exceptionally fair dealing. A high standard of honour should, however, be fixed by the members themselves and stead-
(p. 108)	fastly adhered to. The Incorporated Law Society should inquire into cases of general malpractice as above defined, and should
(p. 110)	be empowered to administer a caution or public reprimand for unprofessional conduct, and to suspend a solicitor from practice for a certain period for dishonourable transactions.

III. Insolvency and Malpractice on the part of Fiduciary
Agents other than Solicitors.

Solicitors are not the only persons who act in a fiduciary capacity. Stockbrokers, executors, auctioneers, and accountants, are often entrusted with other people's money. Treating of such persons, allusion is more particularly made to accountants, acting as professional trustees, official liquidators, &c., who unlike solicitors are not required to possess any recognised qualifications or professional status. Owing to the facilities afforded for evading the requirement of "security" on being appointed to the office of trustee, creditors have suffered losses in some instances by these persons appropriating large sums of money to their own use. The laxity of the procedure for administering the property of liquidating debtors, is a direct encouragement to malpractice and fraud on the part of the trustees who are practically uncontrolled. Then, again, there are auctioneers appropriating to their own use the proceeds of their clients' property; stockbrokers receiving moneys for investment and retaining them; under-sheriffs improperly detaining proceeds of executions, &c.
Mr. Wreford (p. 35)
(p. 36)
(p. 37)
(p. 36)
Mr. Mills (p. 72)

Auctioneers and accountants frequently have recourse to the Bankruptcy Court for relief from debts, and it is calculated that the proportionate number of failures of auctioneers is twelve times, and of accountants six times greater than that of solicitors.
Mr. Wreford (p. 36)
Mr. White (pp. 100, 101, & 103)

In regard to defaults of fiduciary agents generally, it is considered that the public interests are already sufficiently protected by the penalties attaching thereto, but, to guard the interest of creditors against malpractice on the part of agents employed to administer insolvent estates, professional trustees should be imperatively required to furnish a general security to the Court of Bankruptcy for the due performance of their trust, and to have their names registered on payment of a certain fee. And for the further protection of the funds entrusted to them, it should be provided that all moneys not actually required for current expenses in the winding up of the estates should be paid into the Bank of England to the credit of the accountant in bankruptcy. The interest derivable from
Mr. Wreford (p. 41)
(p. 44)
(p. 45)

Mr. Wreford — these unemployed funds should be applied in defraying the expenses of the Bankruptcy Court, to the relief of estates from the fees now charged against them, for maintenance of the judicial establishment.

IV. The Prevalence of Sharp Practice in Business and Professional Matters, and the State of Public Feeling in reference to Fraud.

Mr. Wreford (p. 37) — The facilities for malpractice afforded by the laxity of the law produce a bluntness of moral feeling and an eagerness to make money by tortuous ways. "Commissions" are exacted at every turn, especially in regard to the employment of trustees and other agents in bankruptcy matters. (pp. 37 & 38) By an improper use of voting powers in such matters, estates suffer, and pecuniary advantages are secured by professional men at the expense of those whose interests are entrusted to them.

Mr. Smith (p. 90) — There is a general laxity of judgment on the part of the public with regard to fraud, for, while it is admitted in the abstract that fraud ought to be punished, the mildest proposals to punish will be found in wide commercial circles needlessly severe. Commerce is honeycombed by the system of "Commissions" that is, bribes to agents to betray trusts. (p. 89) A certain bastard kind of sympathy is shown towards a trader or professional man who mixes a little fraud with his business operations, the public forgetting that illicit gains do not increase the wealth of the community, and if the business did not go into the hands of a dishonest man, it would probably go into those of an honest one. By increased punishment the present temptation to fraud would be removed. (p. 91) There is no justification of the different measures meted out to fraud and theft, because fraud is nothing but diluted theft, and, although the former obtains the consent of the victim, the injury arising (p. 92) therefrom is in some cases greater than that from a direct theft.

Public opinion is much sooner available against thieving than (p. 93) against cheating, but fraud ought to be branded with its proper name, no matter how many people practise or connive at it. (p. 94) Combined action against fraud becomes absolutely necessary when owing to the complexity and size of modern societies, common report ceases to give the requisite warning against rogues. The proper remedy for fraud is complete publicity, and fraud should be met and defeated by the public authority with as much care and determination as theft.

Mr. SMITH.
(p. 93)

V.—THE PROGRESS OF INSOLVENCY AMONG SOLICITORS, AS SHOWN BY THE STATISTICS, AND CAUSES OF FAILURES.

In dealing with this point, it is necessary to refer to the correspondence previously alluded to, as that correspondence embraces the statistics furnished by Mr. Munton, which have been generally adopted by the writers of the essays as the basis of their comments. These statistics show that the total number of solicitors who failed between 11th October, 1861, and 31st December, 1876, was 810, being an annual average of 54. The annual numbers varied from 16 in 1870, to 101 in 1867, and Mr. Munton estimates that the 810 failures represent about 5 per cent. of the solicitors appearing in the *Law List*.

The statement as to the percentage of bankrupt solicitors, although incredible, is nevertheless true. Many have failed a second time, some even three, four and five times. In the hurry of modern life the fact of a solicitor's insolvency is soon forgotten and he obtains fresh clients. Frederick Dimsdale was trusted on all hands, even by brother professionals, and yet he had passed through the Bankruptcy Court no less than four times. Solicitors rarely have occasion honestly to fail. They are not exposed to losses such as traders suffer from, and although a genuine failure may arise from the fraud or negligence of partners the proportion of such failures is infinitesimal. The variation of the numbers failing in the different years, shows that nine-tenths of the failures were dishonest, and that consequently, nine out of every ten of the defaulters should either have been suspended from practising for a time or struck off the roll. As the number of solicitors tends to increase annually, the number of insolvents would naturally show a corresponding increase, but such is not the fact. In 1869, the

Mr. ROUND
(p. 8)

(p. 9)

(pp. 12, 13, & 14)
(p. 10)

(p. 12)

(p. 13)

Mr. ROUND	last year of the 1861 Act, the number of failures were ninety-four, while in 1870 the first year of the 1869 Act, the number was sixteen. No reason can be given why there should have been one more failure in 1869 than in 1870. As solicitors are not influenced by vicissitudes of trade, it follows that the great majority of those who failed in the former year must have done so dishonestly. The small number in 1870 must be attributable to the Act of 1869, which prevented the enormous number of voluntary bankrupts which is noticeable under the Act of 1861. Solicitors in 1870 apparently dreaded the operation of the new Act, and had not then discovered "the new way to pay old debts" provided by the liquidation clauses of that Act. But as soon as these clauses got into working order the number of insolvent solicitors began to show a steady increase. As so large a number of solicitors who take the benefit of the Bankruptcy Acts do so dishonestly, it is necessary to protect the public against fraudulent bankruptcy on their part.
(p. 12)	
(p. 13)	
(p. 12)	
(p. 12)	
(p. 13)	
(p. 17)	
Mr. WREFORD (pp. 26 & 27)	From actual examination of the Bankruptcy Registers, it is found that the total number of solicitors' failures gazetted between 11th October, 1861, and 31st December, 1877, was 942. These failures relate to 778 individuals, 112 of whom appear more than once, and one of them as many as nine times.* There were 201 failures under the deed clauses of the 1861 Act, and 210 under the liquidation clauses of the 1869 Act, during a similar period of time, while under the former Act there were 423 bankrupts, mostly on their own petition, and under the latter only 108, the power of a debtor to petition against himself having been withdrawn. The general result arrived at is practically the same as that shown by Mr. Munton's figures, viz. :—That five per cent. of the solicitors now appearing in the *Law List*, have at some time or the other within the last sixteen years availed themselves of the operation of the bankruptcy law.
(p. 28)	
(p. 27)	
(p. 29)	
Mr. WHITE (pp. 100 & 101)	The result of an examination of the Bankruptcy Registers for two years, as a test of the comparative accuracy of Mr. Munton's figures, shows there is no ground for the statement that the bulk of solicitors' failures is on their own petition. In the two years (1874 and 1876) thus examined, there were thirty

---

* This gentleman is now undergoing a sentence of penal servitude for felony.

liquidations (debtors' petitions), against thirty-one bankruptcies (creditors' petitions). But for the same two years another writer gives the following figures:—Liquidations fifty-six, bankruptcies thirty-four. With reference to the causes of solicitors failing, it is alleged that the bankruptcy of solicitors results chiefly from fraud or business ineptitude, and but rarely from misfortune, such as the fraud of a partner, and it is asserted generally that the insolvency of solicitors is admittedly less excusable than that of traders.

Mr. WREFORD (p. 26)
Mr. SMITH (pp. 87 & 88)
(p. 94)

The bankruptcy of solicitors is attributable to their embarking in trade speculations, but instances occur now and then in which a solicitor's bankruptcy is due to pure misfortune.

Mr. MILLS (p. 74) (p. 75)

Mistaken confidence on the part of solicitors in the integrity or discretion of their clients is a fruitful source of insolvency to solicitors. Starting in practice with insufficient capital or little connexion is another source, and one that may be perfectly honest. The mere fact of a solicitor investing spare capital on a reasonable speculation affording a fair prospect of success ought not in itself to stamp a failure as dishonest.

Mr. WHITE (p. 101)

VI. THE BEARING OF THE BANKRUPTCY LAW ON THE QUESTION OF THE INSOLVENCY OF SOLICITORS.

The Bankruptcy Act, 1861, rendered the evasion of just debts easy, and solicitors took full advantage of the facilities afforded by it for obtaining release from debts. The Act of 1869 was intended to correct this defect, but in this object it has only partly succeeded, as its liquidation and composition clauses enable dishonest debtors to evade their obligations with impunity. From the time those clauses got into working order the number of insolvent solicitors has shown a steady increase over the small number who failed in 1870.

Mr. ROUND (p. 11)

Under the Act of 1861, solicitors very freely availed themselves of the power of petitioning for adjudication of bankruptcy against themselves, and the withdrawal of this power by the Act of 1869 has had the effect of reducing the number of bankrupt solicitors to an average of one-fourth of the number under the Act of 1861. The abolition of imprisonment for debt

Mr. WREFORD (p. 26)
(p. 27)

Mr. WHEFORD (p. 42) (p. 31) (p. 43) (p. 36) has also tended to decrease the number of insolvent solicitors since 1869, as there is not now so great an inducement for debtors to have recourse to the Bankruptcy Court. The statistics as to insolvency of solicitors under the 1869 Act therefore compare favourably with those under the former Act, but solicitors advising clients under the present Act and seeing how easily payment of debts can be evaded, would naturally not be slow, in case of their own embarrassment, to get rid of their debts on easy terms. The facilities given by the liquidation clauses of the 1869 Act, for obtaining a discharge without reference to any question of conduct or dividend, must result disastrously to the clients of insolvent solicitors, although the Act provides that an order of discharge shall not release the bankrupt from any debt or liability incurred by fraud or breach of trust. The annual number of insolvencies has nearly doubled since the first year of the present Act, the increase being in great measure attributed in the official reports to the ease with which debtors can "liquidate."

Mr. MILLS (p. 68) (pp. 75 & 76) The Insolvency Law, under the operation of which solicitors came prior to the passing of the Bankruptcy Act, 1861, provided that a discharge should not liberate a solicitor from debts due in respect of moneys received for the use of clients and embezzled by or converted to the use of such solicitor. The Insolvency Law, therefore, recognized and enforced the fiduciary relationship existing between solicitor and client, which relationship is overlooked in the Bankruptcy Act, 1869. The statistics published by the Comptroller in Bankruptcy, show that as the working of a Bankruptcy Act gets to be understood, and debtors become familiar with the artifices designed for their benefit, so dividends decrease. The facts shown by these statistics expose the facilities for fraud which the Bankruptcy Law affords, and of which solicitors, among others, take the benefit.

xv.

VII. Proposed Remedies for Checking the Insolvency of Solicitors.

The remedies suggested in the correspondence previously referred to, for checking insolvency among solicitors (in addition to Sir Henry Peek's proposal for giving information in the *Law List*), were:—

1. The appointment of a Vigilance Committee of the Incorporated Law Society charged with the duty of inquiring into cases of bankruptcy, and reporting to the Council, with power to the latter to oppose renewal of certificate if the insolvent solicitor cannot show a case of misfortune.
2. An enquiry by the Incorporated Law Society into the bankruptcies of solicitors, and the compilation by it of a list of insolvents available for reference, which list should distinguish honest from dishonest failures, and be appended to the annual report. The Society also to compel punctual renewal of certificates, and take action in all cases of malpractice.

The pecuniary and personal confidence placed in solicitors demands a remedy against abuse of that confidence, which remedy must come from *outside* the profession, owing to its defective organization and self-government. Laymen must therefore apply the remedy to protect the public. The Judges consider that solicitors should be amenable to special and peremptory discipline, and that the common law is able to furnish that discipline. It would be unfair to go so far as to exclude all bankrupt solicitors from the *Law List*, as an innocent solicitor might thereby be permanently excluded from his profession and means of livelihood, but it is both just and expedient to apply to solicitors regulations of a stringent character, since the statistics of their insolvency reveal a state of facts that demands immediate remedy. As the Courts of Law deal with the misconduct of solicitors in a summary manner, it would be desirable to entrust to a Court of Law—namely, "The London Bankruptcy Court"—the duty of dealing with the question of the conduct of insolvent solicitors. The certificate of any solicitor, who comes before the Court of Bankruptcy, should, at the expiration of

Mr. Round
(p. 6)
(p. 6)
(p. 7)

(p. 14)

(p. 15)

(p. 17)
(pp. 17, 21, 22 & 23)

Mr. Round
(p. 19)

(p. 18)

(p. 18)

(p. 18)

(p. 19)

Mr. Wreford
(pp. 38, 39, & 40)

twenty-eight days from the date of the petition, or such further time as the Court might allow, lapse and determine; and the solicitor should thereupon be precluded from practising, but should have liberty within such period, or afterwards with the leave of the Court, to apply to the London Bankruptcy Court for leave to continue in practice or to renew his certificate; and the Court, after considering the circumstances connected with the insolvency, should have power to grant or refuse such leave, or to suspend him from practice for a certain time, or to strike him off the roll. Notice of any such application by a solicitor should be given in the *Gazette*, and the Registrar of Solicitors, the trustee in the bankruptcy or any creditor should have a right to be heard thereon. It is not proposed to confer these powers on the local Bankruptcy Courts, so that bankrupt solicitors in the country would be compelled to come before the London Court if they wished to continue in practice. It would be necessary for Parliament to confer on the London Bankruptcy Court the requisite powers for carrying out these suggestions. It is considered that the above proposal would not entail much additional work on the London Court, as the provisions would have the effect of greatly reducing the number of defaulters, and of practically putting an end to dishonest bankruptcy. The ground of preference for the London Bankruptcy Court dealing with the question rather than the Incorporated Law Society is that the one is a public tribunal, while the other is a domestic one with no judicial officer. The investigations of the latter would not consequently give satisfaction. The insertion in the *Law List* of the particulars of every solicitor's bankruptcy would work injustice to individuals without affording either information or protection to the public.

Insolvency on the part of solicitors should be dealt with in the following manner :—The Incorporated Law Society should take cognizance of the bankruptcy of any member of the profession. The Registrar of the Bankruptcy Court should be required to notify to the Incorporated Law Society the fact of the bankruptcy, or liquidation, of any solicitor, and if the solicitor fail to produce to the Law Society a certificate of discharge under the bankruptcy or liquidation within twelve months of the date of the petition, then that Society should, through its proper officer, report the failure to the Inland Revenue authorities, and thereupon, the solicitor should be precluded from obtaining a renewal of his certificate. In the event of a solicitor becoming bankrupt a second time, the officer of the Law Society should at once report the insolvency to the Inland Revenue authorities, so as to prevent renewal of certificate. If a discharge should be obtained under a second bankruptcy, or, after the expiration of twelve months under a first bankruptcy, then the solicitor should be entitled to apply to the High Court of Justice for readmission as a solicitor. Notice of the application to be given to the Registrar of the Law Society and the trustee of the debtor's estate, who, as well as any creditor, should be entitled to be heard thereon. If readmitted, the Judge's order should be due authority for reissue of certificate. If bankrupt a third time, the insolvent solicitor should be forthwith struck off the rolls. The *Law List* should be the recognized official register, and contain the names of all solicitors taking out certificates up to 31st December in each year. No certificate to be taken out after that date, except in case of new admissions. Any solicitor whose name does not appear in the *Law List*, should be precluded from practising or recovering fees for work done, and should also incur some penalty for so practising. A solicitor allowing an unqualified person to practise in his name should also be liable to some penalty.

As the renewal of a bankrupt solicitor's certificate would, on the adoption of the above suggestion, depend on his obtaining a discharge under his bankruptcy or liquidation, the Bankruptcy Law should be amended so as to make the obtaining of a discharge more difficult than under the liquidation clauses of the Act of 1869. Any amendment of the Bankruptcy Law tending to restrict the existing facilities for liquidating and obtaining discharges would also, naturally, have a beneficial effect in checking insolvency among solicitors. A debtor should not be allowed to avail himself voluntarily of the Bankruptcy Laws, unless he can show tangible assets available for creditors, because "liquidation" with no assets cannot possibly benefit creditors. The majority of creditors required for assenting to the grant of a discharge should be a majority in number and four-fifths in

Mr. WREFORD value of the *whole* of the creditors, not merely of those who may attend a particular meeting. And even when assented to by the statutory majority, the Court should have power to withhold the discharge on specified grounds. Proxies should not be used on the question of discharge, unless expressly given for the purpose, with instructions from the creditors as to the manner of voting.

Mr. HAZARD The proposal to appoint a Vigilance Committee of the Incor-
(p. 56) porated Law Society, to report to the Council on the defaults of members of the profession, is somewhat analogous to the French system of Chambers of Discipline, in which system there are points worthy of consideration when relieved from the
(p. 57) exaggeration of its legitimate objects. The exercise of any vigilance on the part of the general members of the profession is not applicable in large towns. To the absence of autonomy and *esprit de corps* in the profession is attributable the need of more than individual and voluntary restraints on questionable members of the profession. A central committee, formed from the officers and rank and file of the Incorporated Law Society, would operate as an improvement on the French system, as the
(p. 58) the utmost impartiality might be looked for from such a committee, while its action would prove of general benefit to the
(p. 58) profession and the public. Such a committee would, however, be abnormal and liable to fitful action. In reference to the proposal for charging the Law Society with the duty of
(p. 59) enforcing discipline generally it is argued that, as the society holds an effective and responsible office under the Crown, it should be responsible for the due control of the profession, and should be bound to take action on any complaint on oath, not as judge, but as investigator and prosecutor. This procedure would involve the necessity for private action in the first instance, which would be preferable to a Committee of Vigilance
(p. 61) taking the initiative. Bankruptcy should be made a more public and enduring disgrace to the defaulter than it is at present the case, and greater publicity should be given to cases in which solicitors abuse the confidence of their clients and creditors. As bankruptcy may not, of itself, deserve further punishment, an inquiry would be necessary to determine whether the insolvencies deserve branding or other punishment

as frauds. The Incorporated Law Society is the proper   Mr. HAZARD
authority to whom the proposed reforms should be entrusted,   (p. 63)
and the Council should, therefore, seek enlarged powers to meet   (p. 60)
the measures of reform it is expected to undertake and endeavour
to identify itself more thoroughly, than at present, with the   (p. 63)
legal profession. The Law Society should also have authority   (p. 62)
over the annual publication of the *Law List*, so that the Registrar
of solicitors might have entire control over the register of that
body. The *Law List* might then contain for the information of
the public a list of the names of solicitors annually suspended
or struck off the roll, or on whom severe penalties may have
been imposed.

The proposal that the Incorporated Law Society should   Mr. MILLS
inquire into the circumstances attending the insolvency of   (pp. 69 & 70)
solicitors and keep a list distinguishing the unfortunate from
the fraudulent would not be practicable, as a public enquiry
would be necessary in order to obtain reliable information, and
this the society could not undertake. The objections would
equally apply to the working of a Vigilance Committee. The
list when prepared would not be accessible to the general
public, and the proposal to give information in the *Law List* is   (p. 77)
open to the same objection. Removal from the ranks of the
profession ought to be peremptory in all cases where a solicitor
is bankrupt, and he ought not to be reinstated till his debts
are paid in full. This may seem harsh, but if a man mismanage his own affairs it is positive proof that he is unfit
to conduct those of other people; and, although individual
hardships might arise, the community at large would gain
immensely, and to their welfare alone should the legislature
look. A solicitor ought not to be allowed to rob with impunity   (p. 78)
under the protection of the Bankruptcy Law. The bankruptcy
of a solicitor arising wholly from professional duties would be
robbery at law if there were any means of getting at the
evidence, and if it arise from causes extraneous to his profession
it is clear he cannot live by it and therefore should be
excluded from it. The public welfare demands that bank-   (p. 77)
ruptcy should vacate the seat of a member of parliament, or
town council, and solicitors ought to be brought under a similar
enactment. But provision should be made that the disabilities

Mr. Mills (p. 75) (p. 78) attaching to a solicitor's insolvency should not apply to those members of a firm whose separate estates are solvent. It is not desirable, however, to apply a drastic remedy if gentler means will prevent a recurrence of the disorder, and commiseration should not be excited by excessive severity. The remedy should not, therefore, in the first instance, go the length of striking a bankrupt solicitor off the roll, but although permitted to practise, he should not be allowed to sue for fees or have his name included in the *Law List*, until he can produce a certificate of payment of his debts in full. The result would be, that solicitors who now omit to take out certificates in time for their names to be inserted in the *Law List*, would be especially careful that their names should appear, and the public would also be supplied with an inducement to consult the *Law List*. A bankrupt (p. 79) solicitor would then either honestly discharge his past debts by his professional exertions, or if he found it impossible to do so, would quit the profession for some other calling. The regula- (p. 76) tion of solicitors should be committed to such a body of men as is proposed in the Bill, which has been before Parliament, for regulating the discipline of barristers, and they should have power to remove a solicitor from the roll for grossly improper conduct. Authorized members of both branches of the profession would then be amenable to a competent and impartial tribunal.

Mr. Smith (p. 88) The alterations of the conditions occasioned by the development of locomotion, under which professions are now exercised, necessitates compensatory changes, in order to relieve honesty from disadvantages in the struggle with dishonesty. The public are now compelled, by reason of modern changes, to deal with persons respecting whom no trustworthy information is readily obtainable. Impunity is therefore conferred on dishonesty. As to the remedies suggested for preventing defaults on the (p. 82) part of solicitors, it is doubtful whether the proposal for disciplinary action from within the profession would be efficacious. The interests to be guarded are those of clients and the public, and these would not be safe in the hands of representatives of (pp. 82 & 83) the class whose members imperil them. The Committee of the Stock Exchange, for example, is shown to have been unduly lax in administering the powers it possesses over defaulting members of their own body to the prejudice of the public. Some kind of disciplinary action from within the legal profession would be better than nothing, if there are insuperable objections to the publicity mode of action, and a Council might usefully conduct inquiries necessary for a proper public record. The Bankruptcy Law protects the bankrupt from his creditors; the law, therefore, should provide an easily accessible record of its action in the matter. The record should be a general one and apply to all insolvents and not merely solicitors. But there is difference enough between solicitors and traders to warrant action in case of the former, even if there are difficulties in the way of the latter. The interests entrusted to a solicitor are of a more intimate character than those involved in ordinary commercial relations, his insolvency is, therefore, matter for more stringent treatment. As a complete register of solicitors exists in the *Law List*, the addition to that list of the information respecting bankrupts, proposed by Sir Henry Peek, would have a wholesome effect and would help to put the public on the right track for dealing with fraud generally. Insolvency is a public fact, and there is no reason why the mode of publication should be chosen with regard to the convenience of the insolvent. The remedy is "publicity," and this would be found efficacious in cases of insolvency arising either from fraud or business ineptitude. In cases of pure misfortune the "public record" should contain some qualification of the bare fact of insolvency. A sectional remedy against defaulting solicitors ought not to be sought, but this question offers a good opportunity for initiating an attack on prevalent commercial fraud, and the recklessness which can, with difficulty, be distinguished from it.

Mr. SMITH
(p. 83)

(p. 85)

(p. 86)

(p. 84)

(p. 94)

(p. 86)

(p. 87)
(p. 93)

(p. 94)

It cannot be shown that exceptional legislation is required in reference to the insolvency of solicitors for the protection of the outside public, either on the ground that solicitors are pre-eminently trusted, or that the percentage of failures among them is abnormally large. The average of failures is not greater than that of other professions, and, as compared with auctioneers and accountants, solicitors are an exceptionally solvent class. Insolvency, not dishonest, does not prevent a solicitor from honourably carrying on his practice. From a professional point of view, however, dishonest insolvency must

Mr. WHITE
(p. 104)

(p. 103)

(p. 104)

Mr. WHITE be checked, in order to preserve the high character of the profession. Insolvency, where fraudulent appropriation of a client's moneys is proved, is punishable by striking off the roll.

(p. 105) Insolvency, generally, is a matter which affects the solicitor's character as a member of the profession, and is, therefore, a

(p. 106) question of professional discipline. The proper dispenser of that discipline is the Incorporated Law Society, but it is desirable

(p. 108) to appoint a paid officer to make enquiries, rather than to entrust that duty to a Vigilance Committee. This officer should report to the Council of the Society, which should consider and decide on the matter. The Council should have power to consider, whether the failure is honest, or culpable, or dishonest.

(p. 110) If culpable, it should have power either to caution the defaulter, or suspend his certificate for six months; if dishonest, the suspension might extend for three years; but if it exceed six months, an appeal should be allowed to the Presidents of the Divisions of the High Court of Justice. Necessary powers to enable the Council and its officer to carry out these suggestions should be conferred by an Act of Parliament. It would be

(p. 111) better for the profession to reform itself, than to leave it to outsiders; and in reforming themselves, solicitors will benefit the community at large.

FIRST PRIZE.

Mr. HERBERT T. ROUND, LL.B., B.A.

ATTENTION has lately been directed, both in Parliament and in the Public Press, to what may not unfairly be called the progress of insolvency amongst Solicitors, and to the disasters which so often fall upon many innocent members of the community as the direct result of these legal failures. It may, therefore, be well to inquire whether some remedy for this evil is not accessible, and, if so, what form that remedy may most conveniently take.

Now, scarcely anyone will deny that solicitors stand in an altogether special and peculiar position, both as to their part in the administration of justice and the management of the *minutiæ* of "adjective" law, as to their special privileges and monopolies, and last but not least, in that there is probably no other body of men, concerning whose qualifications, organization, and duties, the general public know so little and display so slight an interest. Speaking roughly, everyone is aware that his medical man may be a Doctor of Medicine or merely an ordinary surgeon, and that his parish clergyman is a graduate of such and such an university or college, but how many Englishmen know or care in what manner their solicitor became qualified, where he was trained, what privileges he has, and to what government he is subjected. Into the reasons for this lack of interest it is not now our province to enter, but it may be desirable to note that such apathy has in great part tended to cause that special want of organization and self-government which is displayed by the body of solicitors.

One sentence, however, as to the privileges of solicitors may be useful. In England and Wales, of which alone this essay treats, the whole of the legal work (subject only to very minute exceptions) passes in some way or other through the hands of one or more of those persons who are now all comprised under the generic title of "Solicitors of the Supreme Court." Of course we do not ignore the existence of Trade Protection Societies, County Court "Agents," and such like channels through which a portion of the legal or quasi-legal waters make their way ; but not one of these can lawfully issue a single writ or summons, prepare (for reward) a single deed, or advocate a single cause without the intervention of a duly-qualified solicitor.

Nor must it be forgotten that the peculiarity and complexity of legal proceedings causes a client to be much more within the power of a solicitor than is the case with any other profession. There are very few cases in which a doctor may not be given up and a new surgeon or physician consulted whenever the patient so desires. But, this is far otherwise in the case of a solicitor, for the papers and documents connected either with an action or with conveyancing business, are in general absolutely essential to the carrying on of the matter, and in cases of any importance, days, or even weeks, must pass before the new lawyer can both get possession of the necessary papers, and sufficiently master their contents, to be able adequately to represent the interests of his client ; whilst for this last service he must charge heavily, if the very considerable time necessary for much tedious perusal and consideration is not to prove unremunerative. Then there is to be considered the unique combination of pecuniary and personal confidence which is placed by the public in the majority of solicitors, and which trust, it is only fair to say, is in a large number of cases fully justified. Yet, the undeniable fact of the existence of many exceptions, and that too it is feared in increasing numbers, spreading distress and ruin throughout the circle over which their influence extends, seems at once to justify the public in demanding some remedy, and the great body of solicitors themselves in assisting to carry out that very proper demand. For reasons into which this is not a fitting place to enter at length, it is useless to expect that any sufficient remedy will be supplied inside the profession. Nor must it be understood that any reflection is implied hereby upon the individual members of the body of solicitors, but their organization and powers of self-government are partly defective and partly allowed to remain in abeyance on account of difficulties in their working. Laymen themselves should, therefore, apply the remedy, and we shall conclude this essay by the suggestion of a means which appears to us to go as far as is at present practicable towards the protection of the public.

Before, however, proceeding to the more immediate consideration of the legislation which we would propose, it may be well to point out that the principle upon which our arguments are based—namely that of special remedies applicable to the special status of solicitor—already exists in the Common Law, and has on more than one occasion been vigorously applied by the Courts. If some of the most eminent judges of the day consider, not only that solicitors ought to be amenable to very special and peremptory discipline, but that the principles of the Common Law are actually capable of furnishing such discipline, we shall hardly be considered out of place in suggesting some modifications in the direction of practicability and effectiveness of that protection which men so able have extended to the public. Nor must it be thought that the great majority of solicitors themselves are averse from such a course as that which we propose. On the contrary, if we are to judge from the tone of the journals which represent the interests of the profession, the very reverse is the case. One editor says:—"We should like to see the names of all bankrupt solicitors excluded from the *Law List*, were it not that such a step might work considerable wrong;" a remedy which would be very much stronger than can be fairly argued for, since it would consign an insolvent solicitor, howsoever innocent he might be, to a permanent exclusion from his profession and means of livelihood. Other legal editors, as also the great majority of their correspondents, follow in the same strain, and indeed throughout the whole of the comment and discussion which the subject of our essay has undergone in the legal press, not one voice, so far as we know, has been uplifted against some action being taken in the direction which we are pointing out. The universal cry is, "something must be done," "we must face the difficulty," "we hope the matter will be taken up," "the question is, what shall these means be?" and much more to the like effect.

All these expressions it must be borne in mind are taken from the articles and letters of solicitor-editors and writers; the suffering public speak much more strongly (although they may not have a clear understanding of the evil and its remedy), as the following extract from a letter appearing in *The Echo*, of February 18th, 1878, will show. "The alarming increase of defaulting lawyers (meaning solicitors) is due partly to the supply of lawyers being very greatly in excess of the demand, but principally to the now notorious custom, winked at by the Law Society's Council, of all sorts of rascals practising in pettifogging solicitors' names who absorb large profits which would otherwise come to admitted solicitors." And the writer then suggests certain means which he thinks "might be to the advantage of suffering and illtreated clients and creditors now without hope or redress."

Here let us say one word as to the scope of this essay. We purpose confining our attention simply to the question of insolvency. The question of malpractice, as distinguished from bankruptcy, is one which appears not only to be essentially different in its nature, but to demand treatment so entirely diverse, that its proper discussion would be impossible within the limits of this essay. Bankruptcy is a definite fact; malpractice is matter of opinion and highly indefinite, and the cause which we have at heart, the protection of the public from insolvency on the part of solicitors, would, so far at least as legislation is concerned, be seriously injured by entanglement with the question of malpractice.

We will now shortly review some of those curious and highly interesting statistics, the accidental revelation of which has been the means of calling attention to our subject.

That one out of every sixteen solicitors now in practice, has been at some period publicly bankrupt,[*] seems a startling and improbable statement, yet, not only is this true, but a very considerable number of the insolvents have failed a second time, some even repeating the operation as much as three and four times during their professional career, whilst there is actually at this moment in practice, a solicitor who has passed through the Bankruptcy Court no less than five times in the last fifteen years. It might well be thought that such an extraordinary number of failures would work its own cure, that the insolvents would quit the profession, and that no one would ever think of becoming the client of a man who had failed twice, even if he took the risk of placing his affairs in the hands of one who had once been a bankrupt. But, unfortunately, these

---

[*] The word "bankrupt" is here, and sometimes elsewhere, used in its popular sense, as signifying any evasion or relief of debts by virtue of the Bankruptcy Acts.

are not by any means found to be the facts. In the hurry of modern life many things are forgotten, many overlooked, which would probably not have shared those fates thirty, or even twenty years ago, and very little consideration is necessary to convince oneself that such is the case. The history of Frederick Dimsdale, late an apparently wealthy and respectable solicitor of the City of London, but now undergoing a life sentence of penal servitude would, in itself, be almost sufficient to prove our proposition. This man, of whom, according to the authority of the principal legal journal, "not one in two hundred solicitors suspected the honesty and standing," and whose frauds and forgeries involved scores of innocent persons in loss, distress, and even ruin, had actually passed through the Bankruptcy Court no less than four times, and two out of the four within fifteen years of the time of his exposure and conviction. And to show in a concrete form how easily the insolvency of such men escapes notice, a most astute and careful City solicitor and one who had actually practised in London for upwards of twelve years, on hearing of Dimsdale's exposure, said to the writer, " If Frederick Dimsdale had asked me to lend him £100, I would have done so without taking a receipt or any security."

There was nothing whatever, save only the enormity of the fraud, to make Dimsdale's an exceptional instance, and it is beyond all doubt the fact that scores, in all probability hundreds, of solicitors who have been through the Bankruptcy Court under dishonourable circumstances, are now in practice, trusted and unsuspected by thousands of clients and of their fellow-solicitors.

And here, a word as to those members of the profession who fail through genuine misfortune, or through the frauds of partners or other uncontrollable circumstances. First, then, it is our firm opinion, and for which hereafter we shall give statistical reasons, that the number of these genuine failures (as they may be called) is infinitesimal. The very nature of a solicitor's profession excludes those losses which the most experienced of traders may occasionally incur, and his business experience ought to guard him from those bubble speculations wherein the savings of doctors and clergymen are sometimes dissipated. There remain only the fraud or negligence of partners and those very rare and special circumstances which will occasionally fall upon even a careful lawyer, as causes of what we have called genuine failure, and, as might indeed have been expected, the statistics show clearly enough that the number of these bears a wonderfully small proportion to the whole number of solicitors failing in any one year, and a mere fractional percentage to the whole number of solicitors in practice at any one time.

And now for our statistics, which have certainly startled the profession more than they have surprised the public, who are too much accustomed to look with disfavour upon a hardworking and generally honourable profession, on whom it would be conferring no inconsiderable favour to clear it of its black sheep.

It was not until the Bankruptcy Act of 1861 that solicitors (and professional men generally) became amenable to the action of this class of Acts and entitled to their privileges, and from the time that Act came into force (October 11th, 1861) up to the end of 1876, there were 810 failures of solicitors notified in the *Gazette*, being an average of 54 in each year. But this average has varied in a manner which seems to show beyond a doubt, that something like nine-tenths of such failures were dishonest, and that consequently nine out of every ten of those who so failed ought to have been struck off the Rolls, or, at least, suspended from practising for a time.

The following table shows in a compact form the details of these 810 failures, together with other useful comparative information:—

Year.	Total number of Solicitors taking the benefit of the Bankruptcy Acts.	Total number of other persons taking the benefit of the Bankruptcy Acts.	State of Trade from *The Economist*.	REMARKS.
1862	83	12,231	Good	Annual average of failing Solicitors under the Act of 1869 = Seventy-Seven. (The 1862 returns include 14½ months.)
1863	60	11,426	Improving	
1864	61	10,807	Very good	
1865	59	13,450	Prosperous	
1866	65	13,520	Bad	
1867	101	15,805	Bad	
1868	93	17,147	Fairly good	
1869	94	14,970	Good	The Bankruptcy Act, 1869, came into operation 1st January, 1870. Annual average of failing Solicitors under the Act of 1869 = Twenty-Eight.
1870	16	4,986	Good	
1871	29	6,259	Good	
1872	21	6,814	Good	
1873	25	7,464	Declining	
1874	31	7,888	Indifferent	
1875	34	7,855	Bad	
1876	38	9,211	Bad	
15 years	810	159,833	Total annual average of failing Solicitors .. 54	

This table is well worthy of study by all who are interested in the honesty of solicitors—and who is not?—as well as by all who would understand the effects of recent bankruptcy legislation. Before, however, we come to consider the deductions from these statistics as to the pecuniary morality of solicitors, a few explanations may be desirable.

The Bankruptcy Act of 1861 rendered the evasion of just debts easy, and the Act of 1869 was intended to correct this effect in which, however, it has only partially succeeded. The 1869 Act is still in force, its "liquidation" and "composition" clauses being those under which dishonest bankrupts evade their debts with impunity. About 1872-1873 these clauses began to get into working order, and the number of solicitor insolvents shows from that time a steady increase.

The above statistics are taken, as to solicitors, from Mr. Munton's investigations, published in the *Solicitors' Journal*, of March 16, 1878, and of the substantial accuracy of which there can be no doubt, and as to the public, from the annual reports of the Chief Registrar of the Court of Bankruptcy, and from the "General Report by the Comptroller in Bankruptcy, for the year ending 31st December, 1877." This general report is remarkably able and instructive, and its perusal is heartily commended to those interested in present bankruptcy legislation.

The state of trade in the different years is deduced from the Annual Supplement of *The Economist* for the, respective years.

It is desirable to note that the numbers of bankruptcies, both solicitor and public, from 1862 to 1869, include arrangements under "Trust Deeds," a method of evading just debts provided by the Act of 1861, and very largely resorted to, but now happily abolished. The enormous number of bankrupts under the old Act was principally due to this provision, a statement which is made sufficiently clear when it is borne in mind that in 1868, with 9,195 bankruptcies, there were 8,045 trust deed arrangements; whilst in 1869, against 10,396 bankruptcies, there were only 4,668 trust deeds; the Bankruptcy Amendment Act of 1868 having made their use much more difficult after October 11th, 1868. The yearly increase in the number of insolvencies has always happened under the "Trust Deed" or "Liquidation" clauses of the respective Acts, and to give some idea of the nature of this increase, in 1862 there were according to the before-mentioned reports, 2,651 trust deeds, whilst in 1868, the last year of their existence, there were as already stated no less than 8,045, and as to liquidations by arrangement and compositions, in 1870 there were 1,351 bankruptcies and 3,651 liquidations and compositions, and in 1877 only 967 bankruptcies against 8,566 liquidations and compositions, and there can be no doubt that solicitors were at least as quick as the public in discovering this new way to pay old debts.

And now as to the special bearing of these facts upon solicitors : Firstly, it is quite clear that the vicissitudes of trade, and the number of failures amongst the public, have no perceptible influence upon the number of failures amongst solicitors. This is an essential point to establish, since otherwise it might be argued that the 101 solicitor failures in 1867 were caused by exceptional circumstances of trade, or the like. But in that year we see that the number of insolvencies amongst persons other than solicitors was about 15,800; whilst, when 17,147 of the public failed in 1868, only 93 solicitors figured in the list, trade being "fairly good." Still more striking, in 1869, to ninety-four insolvent solicitors there are 14,970 other insolvents; whilst in 1870 there are but sixteen insolvent solicitors to nearly 5,000 other bankrupts, a decrease of *two-thirds* in the one case, and *five-sixths* in the other, trade being "good" in both years. Can anyone doubt that the reason of this is simply because the dishonest solicitors knew and dreaded the new Act very much better than the confiding public ? More elaborate consideration of these facts would only tend to confirm the proposition we have now established, and we will therefore pass to a special consideration of the solicitor column of the above table.

Here the average yearly number of failures from 1862 to 1876 is fifty-four, but as the number of solicitors tends to increase every year, and was in 1876 quite 20 per cent. more than in 1862*, we ought to find the number of failures somewhere about fifty in 1862, and gradually rising up to about sixty in 1876. Commercial crises, "black Mondays," and the like, do not, as might have been expected, and as the above considerations show, influence more than a very small fraction of solicitors, for many of whom, indeed, such trade disasters actually make work. It

---

* A careful estimate from the Law Lists of these years makes the increase over 26 per cent. This only strengthens the argument.

is not to be supposed that the loss of a few bills of costs will drive an honest solicitor, even though he be poor, into the Bankruptcy Court; how then are we to account for the extraordinary fluctuations in the above table? Simply by the fact that something like fifty out of every fifty-four of the annually failing solicitors pass through the Court dishonestly, and not on account of any reasonable excuse or misfortune. From this conclusion we see no escape. Why should the numbers vary from 59 to 101 during the period in which the easy-going Bankruptcy Act of 1861 was in force, when there were many less solicitors than there are now, and the average, assuming all the failures in the solicitors' column of the above table to be honest, and making allowance for the difference in the number of solicitors, should have been about fifty instead of seventy-seven? This difference shows clearly enough that no less than twenty-seven dishonest solicitors passed through the Court annually, so that at the end of the eight years there would be more than 200 bankrupt solicitors in practice. Of course, some allowance must be made for deaths and for the few who may have left the profession, but after every deduction which can be suggested, we cannot escape the conclusion that at the least 150 rogues were allowed to continue to prey upon society. Nor is the worst yet told, for during the seven years from 1870 to 1876 the annual average of failures is actually only twenty-eight as against (approximately) fifty-eight, which might have been expected had the whole 810 failures been due to genuine misfortune, and, still more astounding, in the year 1870 the total number of failures was actually only SIXTEEN as against NINETY-FOUR in the previous year. We are unable to discover any reason whatever except the one already noticed and again to be referred to—why there should have been one more bankruptcy amongst solicitors in the year 1869 than there was in the year 1870? But this extraordinary difference in number is, we have no doubt whatever, due entirely to that one cause, namely, that in 1870 the Bankruptcy Act of 1869 came into force, a measure which was at least intended to check, and which to some extent seems to have succeeded in preventing, the enormous number of what may be called voluntary bankrupts. It was, in short, found that under the Act of 1861, almost any dishonestly inclined person might obtain a release from his debts, even although there was a reasonable probability of his being able to pay them, and dishonourable solicitors seem to have taken full advantage of this; whilst the Act of 1869 put a stop for a time to so easy a method of escape from just obligations.

None know so well as solicitors the dangers and difficulties which beset the working of new legislation, and instead of about ninety-six presenting themselves to the Court for the process of release, not more than sixteen came forward, a fact which seems to show with the utmost clearness, that at least eighty in each year out of the 101, 93 and 94 who failed in the preceding years did so dishonestly.

The importance of these figures cannot well be exaggerated. They show that every recurring year there are about eighty out of say 12,000 solicitors who are dishonest enough to wish unjustly to evade their creditors, and if ready to descend to such degradation, then very surely prepared also to fleece their clients whenever they can safely do so, having regard to the exigencies of the Criminal Law; eighty a year; eight hundred in ten years; making allowance for deaths and other vacancies, say seven hundred out of a total of about 12,000 solicitors, so that calculated upon misfeasance (actual or potential) in the matter of Bankruptcy alone the chances are only, on the average, fifteen to one against every person who consults a solicitor falling into the hands of a dishonest man.*

And now having sufficiently shown that the facts recently brought to light not only require, but in the interests of all honest men and not least of honest solicitors, demand immediate remedy, it may be as well to place the principle for which we are contending upon the safe foundation of high legal authority and precedent. This principle, then, may be shortly restated thus: that it is both just and expedient to apply to solicitors legal regulations somewhat more stringent and high pitched than is necessary in the case of the general public.

Now, besides the liability which solicitors, as members of the public, are under, to answer at the proper tribunals for any breach of duty, or for any crime, there is another mode of proceeding against them which applies to solicitors exclusively, and that is by an application to the summary jurisdiction of the Courts. This jurisdiction is exercised according to "law and conscience," is not governed by technical rules, and, in its

---

* It is to be noted that these figures are all under rather than over the mark, by reason of the under estimate upon page 13.

exercise, the Court may punish by way of fine, by attachment, by suspending a solicitor from practising for any period, or by striking him off the rolls. And further, under this jurisdiction solicitors are liable to be summarily dealt with for misconduct by the Courts of Law, although such misconduct arises in a transaction in which the solicitor is not acting in his professional capacity, a principle now well settled, and to be found fully set out in what are known as the text-books. We are, of course, here referring to such conduct as falls short of being an indictable offence. In Archbold's practice (vol i. p. 148) we find :—" The Court will in general interfere in this summary way, and strike an attorney off the rolls or otherwise punish him for misconduct, not only in cases where the misconduct has arisen in the course of a suit, or other regular or ordinary business of an attorney, but where it has arisen in any other matter so connected with his professional character as to afford a fair presumption that he was employed in or entrusted with it in consequence of that character." And in Lush's Practice (p. 320) we read as follows:—"For any gross misconduct, whether in the course of his professional practice, or otherwise, the Court will expunge the name of the attorney from the rolls;" whilst so high an authority as Lord Mansfield, in a case of *ex-parte* Brounsall (Cowp. 829) laid it down that the Court should inquire whether having regard to the conduct of a solicitor in a particular matter, "it is proper that he should continue a member of a profession which should stand free from all suspicion." To the same effect is Baron Alderson (Stephens *v.* Hill, 10 Mee. & W. 28) who says :—" The question in this case is, whether the attorney has so misconducted himself in his character of attorney as to be an unfit person to remain on the rolls. If persons are to be accredited by the Court it is our duty to watch over and control their conduct." And Lord Ellenborough is even stronger (Rex *v.* Southerton, 6 East 126), when after the Court had held that a defendant had not been "guilty of an indictable offence," he says :—"Enough appears to the Court to satisfy them that the defendant is a very improper person to remain as an attorney upon the rolls of the Court," and the defendant was accordingly struck off the rolls. So Lord Denman (In *re* King, 15 L.J., Q.B. 2) states that "the question to be decided in these cases is not whether a solicitor has been guilty of an indictable offence, but whether he has been guilty of so great a moral fraud as to render him unfit to continue an officer of the Court." And in more recent cases the principle has been laid down with even greater distinctness. Thus (In *re* Blake, 30 L.J., Q.B. 32), Lord Chief Justice Cockburn gave judgment to the following effect :—"Where an attorney is shown to be guilty of gross fraud, although it may not be such a fraud as may make him subject to criminal proceedings, and although the fraud was not committed by him while the relation of attorney and client was subsisting between him and the person defrauded, or in his character of attorney, yet still, in such a case where one who is an officer of the Court has been guilty of gross fraud, we are called upon for the protection of suitors and others who would give credit to him as an attorney to visit such misconduct with summary punishment." And in the same case Justice Wightman said:—" It is of the greatest importance that transactions in which attorneys are parties should be *uberrimæ fidei*, and that those who are accredited as officers of the Court should be above suspicion." In a still later case (In *re* Hill, 37 L.J., Q.B. 295) Lord Chief Justice Cockburn supports his former judgment thus :—" I for one am perfectly prepared to abide by what I said in Blake's case, where you have a solicitor committing a gross fraud, where a man does that which involves dishonesty, it is for the interest of the suitors that the Court should interpose and prevent him from having the opportunity of using his powers when employed in the character of attorney of the Court, to defraud those who obtain his professional services. This is a case in which, although he is not acting in the character of an attorney, yet, as he is an attorney, the Court was bound to take notice of the matter." And Lord Justice Blackburn puts the matter in the clearest possible light when in delivering judgment in the same case, he says :—"We are bound to see that the officers of the Court are proper persons to be trusted by the Court with regard to the interest of suitors, and we ought to look to their character and position and see to what extent they have been guilty of misconduct, and this very much upon the same principle as if we were going to consider, whether or not, they were fit to become attorneys, in which case, if they had previously misconducted themselves, we would consider whether the circumstances were such as to prevent their being admitted, or whether their subsequent good conduct could purge them from it. I adhere to what I think is the effect of Blake's case, that although the misconduct is not directly or incidentally connected with the character of attorney, still we must consider what effect it has upon the attorney being a proper person to be an officer of the Court."

Having now, we think, succeeded in establishing, Firstly—That the enormous majority of solicitors taking the benefit of the Bankruptcy Acts do so dishonestly, and, Secondly—That the principle is well settled, that in the interests of the public the Courts should visit upon solicitors summary punishment, not only in respect of professional misconduct, but also for dishonest conduct in matters other than those done in their professional character, we come to consider by what means the case of insolvent solicitors may best be met, so as to protect the public, as far as possible, from dishonest bankruptcies, and yet not to work injustice in the case of genuine and unavoidable misfortune.

Now, in order to separate the wheat from the chaff, and to detect with accuracy and certainty which solicitors out of the whole number failing are, and which are not honestly, taking advantage of the laws relating to the relief of insolvents, we would suggest means which may be stated in a very few words. We would have it enacted, that every solicitor adjudicated a bankrupt, or filing a petition for liquidation by arrangement or composition (which involves filing a declaration of inability to pay his debts), should within a limited time be obliged to make an application to the London Bankruptcy Court for an order to enable him to continue to practise as a solicitor. The Court should in its discretion consider whether the applicant had been previously insolvent, and also all or any of the circumstances connected with his present insolvency, and it should have the widest powers to refuse to allow the solicitor to practise for such a period as under all the circumstances it might deem just, or, in cases of repeated insolvency, or where the circumstances were of such a nature as to require such a course, to strike the solicitor off the rolls. In order that the Court should be in a position to decide upon the proper order to be made we would have it enjoined upon the Incorporated Law Society to represent in such proceedings the interests of the profession, which, as already shown, are wholly in the direction of clearing its ranks of defaulters, and we would provide through the same society the machinery by which individuals and the public could obtain such information as would enable them to bring to the notice of the Court all particulars with which it should be made acquainted.

Appended to this essay is a short Act, which will give, in greater detail than is here desirable, the means by which these objects might be carried out in the simplest and most effective manner.

No course appears to be so natural, fair, and reasonable, as that the London Bankruptcy Court should inquire into each case as it arises, and pronounce judgment therein. This Court has already official notice of and control over all proceedings instituted in bankruptcy, it is a superior Court of Record, it is entirely above even a suspicion of bias or unfairness, and, to prevent the possibility of injustice, we propose that every facility for appeal should be allowed. Nor let it be supposed that any very great quantity of extra work would by this measure be thrown upon that Court. The sixteen of A.D. 1870 must not be forgotten, and we are fully persuaded that our proposed Act would at once reduce those sixteen to something less than ten, most of whose cases, we will venture to hope, would be so entirely above suspicion as not to occupy more than a few minutes and not to arouse any opposition. In short, it is our firm belief, rendered morally certain as it appears to us upon a fair consideration of the above statistics, that the passing of such an Act would at once put an end to almost all the dishonest bankruptcy of solicitors and the consequent defrauding of their creditors, and not only so, but the proceedings under such an Act would, at one and the same time, weed out of the profession those hardy knaves who might still be disposed to run the risk of the Court and furnish a practical certificate of honesty to genuine misfortune.

A few words will explain why we prefer that the inquiry into cases of insolvency should be conducted by the London Bankruptcy Court rather than by the Incorporated Law Society. The London Bankruptcy Court is a strong and a public tribunal with judges and officers highly paid and of long experience, whilst the Incorporated Law Society is merely a domestic tribunal scarcely touching anything beyond the merest routine, and with no judicial officer. Its investigations would neither satisfy the public, the body of solicitors, nor the bankrupts; nor would the legislature be likely to confer upon it efficient powers of action.

The reasons why these things are so, being lengthy and complicated, cannot well be here set out; nor does it appear to us that such an inquiry is more than very remotely connected with the bankruptcy of solicitors.

It will be observed that in the proposed Act, jurisdiction is given only to the London Bankruptcy Court, although the County Courts now transact a very large share of the total bankruptcy business of the country, and the reason for this will be obvious to the professional reader, whilst for the uninitiated it may be as well to state that local jealousies, religious and political rivalries, favouritisms, and the like, would preclude the fair and efficient working of such an Act in any Court save only one of the principal Courts of Record in London.

The remedy proposed may possibly appear somewhat novel and unusual, but in principle and in fact it is not so. It appears from the Report of the Select Committee upon the usages of the Stock Exchange, that even stockbrokers require the payment by a defaulter of at least one-third of his stock exchange liabilities before he is eligible for re-admission as a member of "the house," unless special reasons are shown tending to exonerate him from blame; and an investigation into each case is made by the committee. Surely, the morality of solicitors should not be lower than that of stockbrokers. It is understood also that accountants are desirous of setting up some analogous domestic tribunal in the erection and maintenance of which solicitors have so signally failed.

In conclusion, let us notice, very shortly, what objections and suggestions have been hitherto offered in this matter. On January 29, 1878, Sir Henry Peek, desiring probably, rather to call attention to the subject than to suggest any immediate and practicable remedy, asked Mr. Solicitor-General (in effect) whether it might not be desirable to set out in the *Law List* after the name of every bankrupt solicitor, particulars of the date of his bankruptcy, dividends paid, and other similar matters; to which question the Solicitor-General (in effect) replied that he did not think such a course fair or expedient: and we may add, that it would probably be libellous, would be grossly unjust to really unfortunate solicitors, and above all would afford to the public, who scarcely ever think of consulting a *Law List*, neither information nor protection. To this supposed scheme all the opposition and objections of solicitors and others have, however, been directed, and it is perhaps rather unfortunate that Sir Henry Peek's question did not take a somewhat more general form. Not one of these objections stands good with respect to the legislation which we would propose. It reinstates the honest man with the same hand by which it crushes the rogue. It gives no undue publicity to solicitor bankrupts, yet all of them must pass the ordeal; the public are protected as amply and efficiently as is possible by the powers conferred upon the Court; and lastly, the short Act proposed could, without any difficulty whatever, be embodied, if expedient, in the next Bankruptcy Act, which cannot now be long delayed.

(THE STATUTE PROPOSED IN MR. ROUND'S ESSAY.)

THE INSOLVENT SOLICITORS' ACT, 1879.

An Act to impose certain liabilities upon Solicitors adjudicated Bankrupt, or filing in the Bankruptcy Court under the provisions of "The Bankruptcy Act, 1869," a declaration admitting their inability to pay their debts.

WHEREAS it is expedient to amend the law so as to impose certain liabilities upon solicitors adjudicated bankrupt, or filing in the Bankruptcy Court under the provisions of "The Bankruptcy Act, 1869," a declaration admitting their inability to pay their debts:

Be it therefore enacted &c.

1. This Act may be cited for all purposes as "The Insolvent Solicitors' Liabilities Act, 1879," and it shall extend to England and Wales only.

2. In this Act, if not inconsistent with the context, the following terms have the meanings hereinafter respectively assigned to them, that is to say :—

"Solicitor" means solicitor of the Supreme Court of Judicature in England.

"Registrar" means the Registrar of Solicitors.

"Court" means the London Bankruptcy Court.

"Insolvent Solicitor" means a solicitor adjudicated bankrupt or filing in any Court having jurisdiction in Bankruptcy under the provisions of "The Bankruptcy Act, 1869,' a declaration admitting his inability to pay his debts.

"Certificate" means the annual certificate required by law to be obtained by every practising solicitor from the Registrar of Solicitors.

3. From and after the passing of this Act, the certificate held by an insolvent solicitor shall, at the expiration of twenty-eight days from the date of his being adjudicated a bankrupt, or of his filing under the provisions of "The Bankruptcy Act, 1869," a declaration admitting his inability to pay his debts, lapse and determine, and the same shall not be renewed or renewable unless such solicitor shall within the said period of twenty-eight days or such extended time as the Court may from time to time allow, apply to the Court to confirm his certificate, or if the same has expired by effluxion of the time for which it was originally granted, for leave to renew the same, and the Court shall upon such application consider all or any of the circumstances in connection with the insolvency of such solicitor, and inquire whether he has been previously insolvent. If upon such consideration it shall appear to the Court that such insolvency has arisen from circumstances for which the applicant cannot justly be held responsible, or if any other reason which the Court may deem sufficient shall be shown, the Court may make an order confirming the certificate of the applicant, or may give the applicant leave to renew the certificate, or may suspend the certificate, or

may withhold leave to renew the same for a definite time, or until further order, or until certain conditions are complied with, or may order that the insolvent solicitor be struck off the roll of solicitors:

Provided that not less than five clear days before any application is made to the Court to extend the time within which an insolvent solicitor may apply to the Court to have his certificate confirmed, or for leave to renew the same, and not less than fourteen days before any application to confirm or for leave to renew such certificate is made, notice in writing of the application shall be given to the registrar:

Provided that notice of the application to confirm the certificate, or for leave to renew the same shall be given in the *London Gazette* fourteen days at least before the day fixed for the hearing of the application.

4. Copies of all affidavits intended to be used in support of every application made under the provisions of this Act, shall be delivered to the registrar, together with the notices mentioned in the preceding section, or as soon as may be after the delivery of such notices.

5. The registrar may appear by counsel, or solicitor, upon the hearing of any application to confirm or renew any certificate, and upon any other proceeding arising out of or in reference to any such application, and it shall be lawful for the Court to order that the costs, charges, and expenses of the registrar in or about any of the matters aforesaid, be paid by the insolvent solicitor or out of his estate.

6. The registrar shall keep a book in which he shall enter (on payment of a fee not exceeding five shillings) the name and address of any person who shall give notice in writing to the registrar of his desire that notice shall be sent to him of all applications made by an insolvent solicitor under this Act, and the registrar shall, as soon as may be, upon the receipt of any notice from an insolvent solicitor pursuant to this Act, post a copy of such notice to all the persons whose names are so entered in the said book, and such persons or their respective solicitors shall be entitled to inspect, free of charge, during office hours at the proper office of the registrar, the copies of all affidavits which shall be delivered to him respecting such solicitor in manner aforesaid, and also to be supplied by the registrar with copies of such affidavits at a charge not exceeding twopence a folio of seventy-two words.

7. The trustee in bankruptcy, or under a liquidation by arrangement, or composition with creditors of every insolvent solicitor, or any of the creditors of such solicitor may appear in person, or by counsel, or solicitor on the hearing of any application made under this Act, but no person so appearing shall be allowed his costs of or relating to any of the matters aforesaid, unless such costs shall be specially ordered by the Court to be paid to him out of the insolvent solicitor's estate, or otherwise.

8. Any other person desiring to appear upon any application made under this Act shall file an affidavit setting forth the grounds upon which he is desirous or claims to appear, and the Court shall determine whether such person shall be at liberty to appear at that and subsequent applications, but no costs shall be allowed to any person who shall be permitted under this section to appear, unless payment thereof be specially ordered by the Court.

9. If the Court shall be of opinion that the appearance by any of the

persons referred to in sections 7 and 8 of this Act is vexatious, and that the insolvent solicitor or his estate has, in consequence of such appearance, been put to additional expense, the Court may order that the person or persons so appearing shall pay the whole or any part of such additional expense as the Court may deem just.

10. The Court may at any time, upon the application of an insolvent solicitor, and of which application he shall have given five days' notice in writing to the registrar, notwithstanding that the certificate of such solicitor has lapsed and determined under the provisions of this Act, give leave to such solicitor to apply that his certificate be renewed upon such grounds, and under and subject to such terms and conditions as the Court may deem just, and when such leave is obtained the application to renew shall be made under and subject to the same conditions as are hereinbefore provided with respect to such applications made within the period of twenty-eight days from the date of the insolvency, or within such extended time as the Court may from time to time allow.

11. All acts done by an insolvent solicitor within twenty-eight days from the date of his insolvency, or within such extended time as the Court may from time to time allow for hearing the application to confirm or for leave to renew his certificate, shall be of the same force, validity, and effect, as if this Act had not been passed.

12. A solicitor whose certificate expires by effluxion of the time for which the same was originally granted, within twenty-eight days after his insolvency, or within such extended time as the Court may from time to time allow for the hearing of an application to confirm his certificate, may without any leave renew his certificate, but such renewed certificate shall lapse and determine at the expiration of such extended time as the Court may from time to time allow for the hearing of an application to confirm, as if such renewed certificate had been held by the solicitor at the date of his insolvency.

13. Every order made by the Court under this Act shall be subject to appeal, in the same manner and under and subject to the same conditions as shall for the time being be in force with reference to appeals from orders made by the Court.

14. The Lord Chancellor, with the advice of the Chief Judge in Bankruptcy and the Registrar of Solicitors, may from time to time make and from time to time revoke and alter rules for the effectual execution of this Act, and the carrying out of the objects thereof.

SECOND PRIZE.

MR. GEORGE WREFORD.

THERE is no necessary connection between the two subjects which form the heading of this paper. They are coupled together in consequence of being mixed up in a controversy which took place in the early part of the present year. This controversy originated in a question asked in the House of Commons by Sir Henry Peek of the Solicitor-General, touching the desirability of placing some distinguishing mark in the *Law List* against the names of those solicitors who have become bankrupt or insolvent. Following on this question, some articles and letters on the subject appeared in the *Solicitors' Journal*. In these letters assertions were made respecting the number of defaulting lawyers which were called in question by the Editor of that journal. Suggestions were put forward for remedying to some extent the evils complained of, and the controversy ultimately resulted in an invitation in the public prints for contributions on the subject in the form of essays. I propose, therefore, in the following pages, to examine the allegations brought forward, and consider whether any feasible proposals can be made in aid of the object which Sir Henry Peek has in view.

In dealing with the subjects under consideration, I have thought it desirable, in the first place, to inquire how far the allegations made by Mr. Munton in the correspondence referred to are borne out by the official records and registers relating to bankruptcy and insolvency. With this view I have made, at considerable labour, a very careful examination of those records and registers, and the result of my investigations is given in the following table :—

(A.)

Statement showing the number of Bankruptcies and Insolvencies of Solicitors between the 11th of October, 1861, and 31st December, 1877.

YEAR.	SOLICITORS PRACTISING IN LONDON.			SOLICITORS PRACTISING IN THE COUNTRY.			TOTAL.
	Number of Bankrupts.	Number of Deeds.	Total London Solicitors.	Number of Bankruptcies.	Number of Deeds.	Total Country Solicitors.	
Three months 1861	7	..	7	13	1	14	21
1862	31	4	35	39	12	51	86
1863	18	10	28	22	12	34	62
1864	26	10	36	18	8	26	62
1865	20	15	35	24	7	31	66
1866	24	4	28	23	14	37	65
1867	28	28	56	22	17	39	95
1868	25	19	44	22	16	38	82
1869	31	7	38	30	17	47	85
Totals 1861 Act.	210	97	307	213	104	317	624
YEAR.	Bankruptcies.	Liquidations.	Total.	Bankruptcies.	Liquidations.	Total.	TOTAL.
1870	5	17	22	7	9	16	38
1871	6	14	20	10	23	33	53
1872	5	10	15	3	13	16	31
1873	3	8	11	9	14	23	34
1874	4	12	16	8	16	24	40
1875	9	7	16	6	15	21	37
1876	13	10	23	9	18	27	50
1877	8	9	17	3	15	18	35
Totals 1869 Act.	53	87	140	55	123	178	318
Totals 1861 and 1869 Acts.	263	184	447	268	227	495	942

It will be observed from the above table that under the Act of 1861 solicitors very freely availed themselves of the power of petitioning for adjudication of bankruptcy against themselves, most of the bankruptcies having occurred on the debtors' own petitions. There were no less than 210 bankruptcies of solicitors

in London, and 213 in the country during the eight years that
Act was in operation. It will further be noticed that since the
power of a debtor to petition against himself has been withdrawn
by the Act of 1869, that is, during the last eight years, the
numbers have fallen to fifty-three and fifty-five respectively, or
just one-fourth of the numbers under the former system. On the
other hand, it might reasonably be imagined that the number of
private arrangements under the present Act would considerably
exceed the number of deeds under the Act of 1861. But the
increase will be seen to be very slight, the numbers being :—

DEEDS OF ARRANGEMENT (1861 Act)—

London	97
Country	104
Total	201

LIQUIDATIONS (1869 Act)—

London	87
Country	123
Total	210

And the total failures under the 1869 Act are just one-half of
what they were under the 1861 Act during the same number of
years. So that it may be taken as a fact that the state of matters
under the present Act compares favourably with that shown to
have existed under the Act of 1861. And this, notwithstanding
the facilities for getting rid of debts afforded by the liquidation
clauses of the 1869 Act.

The total number of failures shown in Table (A.) are 942, but
this number does not accurately represent the number of persons
failing. In order to ascertain the actual number of individuals
comprised in the 942 cases of insolvency, I have classified the
names alphabetically, and the following Table (B.) shows the
results obtained from this process :—

(B.)

Initial Letter of Name.	Number of Cases under Letter.	Number of Names appearing.				Deduction to be made in respect of Names appearing more than once.	Actual Number of individual Solicitors who have failed.
		Twice.	3 Times.	4 Times.	More than 4 times.		
A.	29	3	...		{ 1 5 times }	7	22
B.	99	7	2	...	{ 1 9 times }	19	80
C.	76	7	...	1	...	10	66
D.	49	5	2	...	...	9	40
E.	35	2	1	...	...	4	31
F.	26	5	...	...	...	5	21
G.	47	2	3	1	...	11	36
H.	79	3	...	...	{ 1 7 times }	9	70
I. J.	22	2	...	1	...	5	17
K.	17	...	2	...	...	4	13
L.	34	3	...	1	...	6	28
M.	63	6	3	...	...	12	51
N.	19	2		...	{ 1 6 times }	7	12
O.	7	1	...	...	...	1	6
P.	76	9	...	1	...	12	64
Q. R.	49	3	...	1	...	6	43
S.	82	9	2	...	...	13	69
T.	36	3	...	1	...	6	30
U. V.	6	1	...	...	...	1	5
W.	87	10	3	...	...	16	71
Y.	4	1	...	...	...	1	3
TOTALS	942	84	18	7	1 each 5, 6, 7 & 9 times.	164	778

The 942 insolvencies are thus seen to relate to 778 insolvents, of whom 84 figure twice, 18 three times, 7 four times, and one each, 5, 6, 7, and 9 times respectively! In dealing with these names I have treated cases in which bankruptcy has followed on failure of liquidation proceedings as single cases of insolvency, they being practically the same failures, though necessarily appearing twice in the *Gazette*.

I find on reference to the *Law List* for 1877, the last year to which my statistics relate, that the number of London solicitors who took out certificates for that year was 3,924, and that the number of solicitors' names appearing under the various country towns was 8,746. But many of the latter practise also in London, or in two or more country towns, under which their names would appear twice or thrice as the case may be. A considerable deduction must therefore be made from the 8,746, and from a calculation I have made, I find that the actual number of country practitioners is about 6,000. This would make nearly 10,000 in London and country. The *Solicitors' Journal* puts the number at 9,000. In calculating the average of failures, I take the former number as less unfavourable to the profession. The 778 defaulters spread over this number of solicitors give an average of 7.78 per cent., or about one out of every thirteen. This indicates a serious state of affairs, but it should be borne in mind that many of the 778 names have, by reason of death, withdrawal from the profession, and other causes, disappeared from the *Law List*. Probably not more than two-thirds of the 778 names appear in the current *Law List*. Assuming this estimate to be correct, the average would be reduced to something like five per cent., or one defaulter in every twenty. Attention having been directed in the correspondence under consideration to the statistics of two particular letters of the alphabet, I have thought it desirable to give more especial attention to these. The result is that the letters referred to, more especially letter "*D.*," exhibit a most unfortunate pre-eminence, as shown in the following table:—

| LETTER. | No. of London Solicitors' Names in *Law List*. | No of Names appearing in *Gazette* | No. of Names appearing. | | Leaving Actual number of Solicitors. | Percentage of Defaulters to Total Numbers. |
			Twice.	Three Times.		
D.	155	34	5	2	25	16.12
W.	325	46	10	1	34	10.46

In reference to bankrupt solicitors, it is a noticeable fact that many of them appear, from their descriptions in the *Gazette*, to have engaged in occupations altogether distinct from and foreign to the profession of the law. To this fact many of the failures are probably attributable.

On the whole, the foregoing figures fully bear out the allegations made by Mr. Munton, and no doubt call for serious attention from those members of the profession who are interested in sustaining its honorable character. But before proceeding to consider what alterations may be expedient in the existing regulations affecting solicitors, or in the present bankruptcy laws, it will be desirable to glance at the changes made in the

bankruptcy laws by recent legislation, that is to say, by the
Acts of 1861 and 1869, especially in reference to the questions
of imprisonment for debt and the abolition of certain distinctions
existing prior to 1861 between traders and non-traders. Before
the Act of 1861, those debtors who came under the denomination
of "traders," as defined by the bankruptcy laws, were entitled
to certain privileges as compared with non-traders. The former
were amenable to and entitled to the benefits of the bankruptcy
law. The latter were amenable to and entitled to such benefits
as were conferred by the insolvency law. The Courts exercising
jurisdiction in bankruptcy were empowered to grant to traders
"certificates of conformity," which certificates had the effect of
discharging the persons and future acquired property of bankrupt
traders from all liability in respect of debts incurred prior to the
grant of such certificates. The Insolvent Debtors' Court, upon a
non-trader surrendering all his property to a provisional assignee,
and making a full disclosure of his estate, was empowered to
grant protection from arrest to the non-trader debtor, but his
after acquired property became liable for payment of his debts.
The difference which thus existed between traders and non-
traders appears to have been a reasonable one. Traders, as a
matter of course, are subject to losses by fluctuations in the value
of commodities, by failures of their debtors, and from many other
causes over which, in many instances, the trader himself cannot
possibly have any control. It seemed only reasonable therefore
that the legislature should step in, not only to protect the person
of the honest but unfortunate trader, but also to make provision
for his release from his debts altogether upon his giving up all
his property for the benefit of his creditors. But with non-traders
the case was essentially different. The failures of non-traders
must, in the majority of instances, be traceable to such causes
as unjustifiable extravagance in living, rash and hazardous
speculation, &c.; and it will be apparent to most people that the
latter would not, as a rule, be entitled to the same consideration
at the hands of the Courts administering the laws of bankruptcy
or insolvency as the former. Up to 1861 this principle was
observable in the legislative enactments. The insolvency laws
were founded on the Act of 53rd George III. c. 102, which
practically remained in operation till Lord Westbury's Bill of
1861 became law. By the Bankruptcy Act, 1861, the distinction
between traders and non-traders, or rather between bankruptcy

and insolvency, was practically abolished. Both traders and non-traders were then made amenable to the bankruptcy law, and for the certificate of conformity an order of discharge was substituted. The grant of this discharge was entirely within the discretion of the Court, subject to the right of creditors to oppose the grant upon showing the bankrupt was guilty of any of the offences specified in the Act. The discharge not only freed the person of the bankrupt from liability of arrest, but also relieved all his after acquired property from any claims by creditors ranking under the bankruptcy. This was felt in many instances to work injustice to creditors, especially in regard to non-traders. In such cases creditors often found their debtors, after getting discharged, possessed of means of paying their debts with no liability on them to do so. This feeling among other causes led to the legislation resulting in the Act of 1869. This Act vested in a certain majority of the creditors the granting of the discharge subject to the approval of the Court. But if the estate pays a dividend of 10s in the £, the debtor is entitled to a discharge as a right, by virtue of the statute. These provisions as to discharge, however, apply only to bankruptcy proper, that is, to adjudications on creditors' petitions. Under the liquidation clauses the creditors are empowered, in case of a debtor's petition and a resolution by the creditors in favour of liquidation by arrangement, to grant, by special resolution, the discharge of the debtor without reference to any question of conduct or dividend. The facility with which discharges can in this manner be obtained, is an important element in connection with the general dissatisfaction occasioned by the working of these liquidation clauses. The advantages which a debtor and his agents acquire over a body of creditors not acting in concert, are so obvious and have been so much discussed, that it is hardly necessary to refer to them here. It is sufficient to indicate that these advantages, when made use of by unscrupulous debtors or their professional advisers, must be disastrous to the interests of creditors; and where the liquidating debtor is himself a professional man, it can easily be imagined how unsatisfactory the results must be to creditors, especially to clients who may have entrusted money or other valuable property to a solicitor, trusting in his professional character.

Although solicitors or attorneys were not considered as traders within the meaning of the bankruptcy laws, they were sometimes brought under the operation of those laws prior to 1861 by coming within the denomination of "scriveners," that is, persons receiving other men's moneys into their trust for purposes of investment, &c. Stockbrokers and others would equally fall within this denomination. It is, however, perhaps hardly necessary to inquire to what extent the legal profession availed themselves of the bankrupt law prior to 1861. The date of the commencement of the Act of 1861 has been fixed upon in the correspondence now under consideration as the starting point for discussion. I have not therefore thought it necessary to carry my investigations back beyond that date. By the abolition of the Insolvent Debtors' Court and the provisions made by the Act of 1861 for periodically clearing the debtors' prisons, by adjudicating the prisoners for debt bankrupt, the number of bankrupts passing through the Court was enormously increased. The abolition of the provision requiring a debtor petitioning against himself to show assets to the amount of £150 tended in the like direction. The facilities afforded by the 1861 Act for either obtaining an absolute discharge from all liabilities, or for effecting arrangements with creditors without recourse to the Court except for purposes of registration, must also be taken into consideration, in looking at the results of that Act. To what extent solicitors availed themselves of these facilities has been fully shown in Table (A.) Under the Act of 1849 the certificate of conformity discharged the bankrupt from all claims and demands made provable under the bankruptcy. But by the Act of 1861 the order of discharge did not release the bankrupt from any debt or liability incurred by means of fraud or breach of trust, and this provision is continued in the Act of 1869.

Although the legal profession is more particularly under consideration in this paper, it must be borne in mind that in the present state of public affairs, solicitors are by no means the only persons who act in a fiduciary capacity. Stockbrokers, auctioneers, executors, accountants (acting as trustees or liquidators) and others are often entrusted with other people's money, as well as solicitors. It will therefore be desirable, in a consideration of the question, how to protect the public so far as possible against malversation on the part of fiduciary agents, to take a broad view of the matter, and not confine the investigation to the treatment of any particular set or class of agents.

Having demonstrated the substantial accuracy of the statements made with regard to the large number of solicitors whose names appear now in the *Law List*, or have appeared there during the last sixteen years, who have, in some form or other, taken the benefit of the bankruptcy laws since the passing of the Bankruptcy Act, 1861; and having also taken a glance at certain changes made in the law respecting the position of traders and non-traders, &c., I now propose to inquire :—

(1.) How far it is fair and reasonable that defaulting solicitors should, amongst other fiduciary agents, be parparticularly singled out for attack, and be held up to public obloquy.

(2.) To what extent persons other than solicitors placed in positions of trust have failed to carry out such trusts in an honorable manner.

(3.) How far the present bankruptcy laws tend to promote a certain laxity of principle in dealing with other people's property.

(4.) Whether in the present state of competition among professional men to obtain business there has not arisen a bluntness of moral feeling in securing personal advantages at the expense of those whose interests they should be bound to consider before their own.

(5.) What means should be adopted, in the interests of the public, and of an honorable profession, for protection against malpractices and defaults on the part of solicitors and others holding themselves out as persons willing to act in positions of trust.

(6.) What alterations may advantageously be made in the bankruptcy laws to further the object mentioned under the previous heading.

1. In regard to the first point, there is no doubt that a general feeling exists among the public, that if a member of the legal profession is convicted of fraud or is guilty of unprofessional conduct, he should be dealt with more severely than an ordinary offender. And it certainly seems reasonable that if the legislature confers special privileges and immunities upon a certain class of men, and puts them in a position for acquiring the confidence and trust of the general public in an especial manner, it should visit with severe punishment any member of that class, who may be convicted before a Court of Justice of a breach of that trust and confidence. The feeling referred to has influenced the higher ranks of the profession

itself, for we find our Judges very outspoken and fearless in their denunciations against frauds committed by solicitors, and they have not hesitated to mete out the most severe punishment when a conviction has been recorded against a member of the profession. I need only mention the recent case of Mr. Dimsdale as illustrative of the point under consideration. But such cases of those of Mr. Dimsdale and Mr. J. A. Jones are fortunately for the honour of the profession of very rare occurrence, or if occurring more frequently than the general public is aware of, are not brought to light. It is rather with cases of a less flagrant character that we have to deal. There are first the cases in which a client entrusts money to his solicitor for safe keeping or investment, and finds that the money has been misappropriated, or in which as more frequently happens, moneys due to clients are received by their solicitors on their behalf, and the clients are afterwards unable to obtain either accounts or money from the solicitors. The law, I understand, gives a solicitor a general lien, on any moneys from time to time in his hands belonging to a client, in respect of any costs due to him. By these means an unscrupulous lawyer has large opportunities of keeping moneys belonging to clients in his hands without bringing himself within reach of the law, or rendering himself amenable to the regulations of the Incorporated Law Society. He has simply to postpone the making out of his bill of costs, and put off the day of settling by frivolous excuses, till the client's patience is exhausted and he threatens proceedings. Then the system of procrastination may be brought to a close, or the client may have still to encounter further vexatious delays, should the solicitor's position be very precarious. In that case, he may either proceed on his own motion to the Court for a rule calling upon the defaulter to show cause why he should not be struck off the rolls, or if he have a very clear ground of complaint, he may perhaps succeed in inducing the Incorporated Law Society to take the matter up. Even then the defaulter's name must not be mentioned in open Court, nor must it appear in the public prints. All the public may be permitted to know is that an application has been made "in the matter of a solicitor." The privileges of members of the profession must not be further trespassed on. Even when it comes to an application of the nature referred to, the defaulting lawyer may still evade any penalty for his misconduct. He may "show cause," file affidavits, apologise, explain, perhaps arrange with the client, and the matter blows over. Cases of misappropriation of moneys entrusted to solicitors for specific purposes are more flagrant, and bring surer and more speedy punishment, provided the defrauded clients make use of the powers of the law, and prosecute the offenders. But cases of this description may and have in many instances gone on for years, and the defrauded clients have been perfectly ignorant of the misappropriation until the death or bankruptcy of the solicitors brings the matter to light. For example, it is by no means an uncommon practice for a lawyer to be entrusted with moneys for investment, with an understanding that the securities shall remain in his custody. This gives an unscrupulous solicitor opportunities of applying moneys to his own use, while pretending they have been invested in certain securities, producing a specified annual income—this income he takes care to pay to, or credit his client with. And so the unsuspecting client goes on till he suddenly finds the supposed securities have no existence. Such cases are doubtless most exceptional, and to the honour of the legal profession be it said, solicitors as a body have most faithfully performed their duties, and have satisfactorily carried out trusts of a most important and responsible character. Where a defaulter of the nature just alluded to becomes bankrupt, too much publicity cannot be given to the matter, his conduct cannot be too severely reprobated, and the public are justified in requiring that due punishment be inflicted on the offender.

2. But solicitors are not the only persons who act in a fiduciary character, and who have improperly carried out the trusts reposed in them. Private individuals, acting as executors or trustees, have sometimes betrayed the confidence of friends. To these I do not now propose to advert. There are persons who make it their *business* to assume responsibilities of a fiduciary nature—persons who advertise themselves as "professional trustees," "official liquidators," &c., and who, unlike solicitors, are not required to possess any recognized qualification or professional *status*, and of whom no "duty" is required to be paid to the State, as in the case of solicitors. They generally "call themselves" accountants, and all they require in order to obtain business is the "confidence" of persons in whom certain statutes have vested the power of appointment to offices of

trust. These offices, unlike ordinary positions of trust, which are of an honorary character, carry with them the right of remuneration to the "trustee" or "liquidator." They are consequently much sought after. In matters of bankruptcy the creditors who appoint a trustee have the power to require him to find security for the due performance of the duties of his office. But this power is very rarely exercised, because, as a rule, the trustee appoints himself by means of the "proxies" of creditors, and by the same means dispenses with the requirement of security. It is hardly to be wondered at then that many defaulters have been found in the ranks of professional trustees. Large sums of money have, in some instances, been appropriated by them to their own use. The trustee perhaps absconds, and his bankruptcy follows. The creditors under the various estates whose management the defaulting trustee may have succeeded in securing, have then to add to their previous losses the further loss occasioned by the trustee's breach of trust. Then, again, there are auctioneers, receiving the proceeds of sales of property belonging to clients, and appropriating them to their own use; stockbrokers, receiving moneys for investment and retaining them and other cases of a like character. I may conveniently mention here that in going through the Bankruptcy Registers for the purpose of ascertaining the statistics relating to solicitors, I was struck with the frequency with which persons described as "accountants" and "auctioneers" have figured in the *Gazette*, especially under the present Act. The statistics in regard to these classes would, no doubt, prove instructive; but they are rather beyond the scope of the present inquiry.

3. The existing bankruptcy law is certainly not calculated to induce people to strain every nerve to pay their debts. The facilities it affords for enabling debtors to rid themselves of their liabilities are so great, that many who would otherwise make every exertion to pay their way are prompted to avail themselves of the process of "liquidation." There is consequently a degree of laxity in commercial morality induced, which a more stringent law might have the effect of eradicating. In a recent official report on bankruptcy matters, it is pointed out that the annual number of insolvencies has nearly doubled since the first year of the present Act. This increase is entirely attributed to the ease with which debtors can evade payment of their debts by "liquidating." Then, again, comes the laxity in administering

what property the bankrupt or liquidating debtor may give up to his creditors. The agents appointed by the creditors to administer such property are, in liquidation matters, practically uncontrolled. By means of the proxies of creditors they determine all questions in which they are personally interested, such as fixing their own remuneration, granting their own release, &c. The laxity of principle induced by such a system, and the malpractices to which such fiduciary agents may almost with impunity resort are sufficiently obvious.

4. This brings us to the consideration of the next point, as the facilities for such malpractices afforded by the law must produce a bluntness of moral feeling and a determination among professional agents to avail themselves of every opportunity of making money by tortuous ways. "Commissions," of which so much has been heard recently, are exacted at every turn. It has even been lately alleged, by a correspondent in *The Times*, that trustees have to be bribed to induce them to admit the proofs of creditors' debts, to enable the latter to receive the dividends to which they are entitled. But this allegation hardly seems credible, except in reference to a fictitious claim. Trustees in bankruptcy matters often have to employ auctioneers to realize property belonging to the estates. They too frequently employ the auctioneer from whom they can extract the largest commission. If the auctioneer's charge were a fixed sum, perhaps the creditors might not suffer. But it is not so. True, a scale of commission on sales is prescribed in the bankruptcy rules; but it is subject to variation by trustees, that is, if the trustee recommend it, the taxing officer may grant an allowance in excess of the scale. The trustee acting for the creditors should keep all charges of agents as low as possible. The trustee, acting in the interests of his own pocket, will recommend as large an allowance as possible to the auctioneer, on the principle that the more he can get the auctioneer allowed, the more will his share of that allowance be. Again, by means of the proxies of the creditors, the trustee, when appointing himself, may appoint a committee of inspection of his own selection —perhaps his partner, or clerk, or some unsuccessful candidate for the office of trustee. To them he may, perchance, delegate the power of the creditors in regard to the granting of his remuneration. There may possibly exist an arrangement between trustee and committee for the latter sharing the former's remu-

neration. In such a case, the committee themselves, acting in a fiduciary capacity, are voting the creditors' money to the trustee, well knowing that the more they vote, the greater will be their share of the so-called "remuneration." In many cases it is out of all proportion to the actual value of the trustee's services, and rightly named, it should be termed "plunder." It sometimes happens that a solicitor holding proxies has practically the appointment of trustee. He appoints, perhaps, not the man best fitted for the office, but the man who will give him the largest share of the remuneration voted to the trustee. The same power which appoints the trustee fixes his remuneration. If the appointing power shares the remuneration, can it be doubted but that estates suffer, and that pecuniary advantages are secured by professional men at the expense of those whose interests they should be bound to consider before their own?

5. The next point involves a wide consideration. In fact, it constitutes the pith of the matter under discussion. In considering the means to be adopted to protect the public against the malpractices and misfeasance of fiduciary agents, I will first deal with what is the more immediate object of this paper—the question of "defaulting lawyers." It has been suggested that all such defaulters should be "gibbeted," by having some special mark put against their names in the *Law List*. I doubt whether the adoption of this suggestion would have the desired effect of protecting the public against untrustworthy members of the profession. The *Law List* is not accessible to the general run of clients. A solicitor is generally recommended by some friend, or his name is known in connection with some matter which has come under the intending client's notice. Seldom is recourse had to the *Law List*. Again by the adoption of the proposed suggestion, no distinction could be drawn between solicitors who may have been unfortunate and compelled to have recourse to the Bankruptcy Court through no fault of their own, and those who may have wilfully betrayed the trusts reposed in them, speculated with their clients' moneys, or embarked in businesses foreign to their profession. Neither is any limit of time suggested in reference to the proposed marking in the *Law List*. On these and other grounds, I am of opinion that the proposed method would not be efficacious, and would be neither just nor reasonable. It seems to me that the matter is one peculiarly for the consideration of the legal profession itself, and the profession

should therefore exert itself for the protection of its own good name through the action of its recognized society—the Incorporated Law Society. Parliament is jealous of its honour and privileges. The legal profession should be the same. How does Parliament act in case of the bankruptcy of one of its members? It suspends the defaulting member from taking part in its deliberations, and in certain circumstances his seat becomes vacant. (See part 5 of "The Bankruptcy Act, 1869"—relating to persons having privilege of Parliament—and also "The Bankruptcy Disqualification Act, 1871.") The legal profession should look to this precedent for an example worthy of imitation and adaptation to the matter under discussion. The desired end might be secured in some such manner as the following :—It should be the duty of the Incorporated Law Society to take cognizance of the bankruptcy or liquidation of any member of the legal profession. In the event of an adjudication of bankruptcy against, or of the registration of a resolution for liquidation by arrangement of the affairs of, any solicitor, it should be the duty of the Registrar of the Court to notify such adjudication or registration officially to the Registrar or other officer of the Incorporated Law Society. The effect of such notification should be that unless the bankrupt or liquidating solicitor should produce to the Registrar or other officer of the society, a certificate of discharge from the bankruptcy or liquidation, or evidence of the annulment of the bankruptcy within say (twelve) months of the date of the adjudication or registration, the Registrar of the society should notify the bankruptcy or liquidation of the solicitor to the Inland Revenue authorities, and thereupon such solicitor should be precluded from obtaining a renewal of his certificate. With regard to the *Law List*, I would make that the basis on which solicitors should be allowed to practise in the Courts or elsewhere. Any solicitor not appearing in the *Law List* should be precluded from practising or recovering any fees for work done. He should also incur some penalties for so acting. Any member of the profession allowing an uncertificated solicitor to act or practise in his name should be liable to some penalty. Solicitors should be compelled to take out or renew their certificates on or before the 31st December in each year, and the *Law List* should be the recognized official register and contain the names of all solicitors taking out certificates up to and inclusive of that date. Exception might be made in case of a solicitor taking out a certificate for the first time. For instance, if a solicitor be admitted at Easter, he should be allowed to practise at once on taking out his certificate, and the production of the certificate should be sufficient authority for his practising in the Courts, signing the rolls, recovering fees, &c., notwithstanding the absence of his name from the *Law List*. With this exception, no certificate should be taken out or renewed except between the 15th of November and the 31st of December in each year. In the event of a solicitor becoming bankrupt a second time, the notification from the Registrar of the Incorporated Law Society to the Inland Revenue authorities should be made immediately on his receiving official intimation of the bankruptcy or liquidation.

If a defaulting solicitor obtain a discharge under a second insolvency, or if he obtain a discharge under a first insolvency subsequently to the expiration of the prescribed period of (twelve) months, or in either case produce evidence of the annulment of the bankruptcy, then he should be entitled to apply to a Judge of the Queen's Bench Division in open Court for readmission to the ranks of the profession. Notice of such application should be given to the Registrar or other officer of the Incorporated Law Society and to the trustee under the bankruptcy or liquidation. These persons, as well as any creditor under the bankruptcy or liquidation, should be entitled to be heard on the application, and the presiding Judge should determine whether the defaulter should be readmitted to the profession. In case of such readmission, the production of the Judge's order should be sufficient authority for the renewal of the certificate. In the event of a *third* insolvency, the defaulter should, *ipso facto*, cease to be a solicitor, and his name should be removed from the rolls of the Court by the Registrar of the Incorporated Law Society.

With regard to defaulters other than actual bankrupts or liquidating debtors, it should be the duty of the Incorporated Law Society to receive complaints of clients or other persons against any member of the profession and to inquire into the allegations; and if the society should be of opinion that the matters complained of are, *primâ facie*, proved, and are of a nature derogatory to the honour of the individual and of the profession generally, it should be the duty of the society to apply to the Court for a rule to strike the defaulter's name off the rolls of the Court. The investigation by the society would necessarily be of a private character; but the application should be public, and the name of the defaulter should not be suppressed. If the complainant should be dissatisfied with the action of the Incorporated Law Society in the matter, he should still have power to apply, on his own responsibility, and at his own cost, to the High Court of Justice for redress, as at present. But it is apprehended that the Law Society would, in all such cases, act as an impartial arbitrator between the public and the profession, and for the honour of the profession would carefully exercise the powers vested in it. As already pointed out, the facilities solicitors possess of getting into their hands moneys belonging to clients, are doubtless the cause of many of the malpractices complained of. It might seem to press unduly on the many trustworthy and respectable members of the profession to endeavour to restrict in any way these facilities. Still I throw out the suggestion for consideration, whether in the interests of the public, solicitors should not be precluded from receiving the moneys of their clients without their client's authority, that is to say, whether a receipt given by a solicitor for moneys due to a client should be a valid discharge to the debtor or other person paying the moneys to the solicitor, without the written authority of the client. Such a provision would enable a client either to prevent moneys from passing into the possession of his solicitor, or to know when his solicitor receives money on his account. It might also be desirable to require solicitors to furnish periodically to clients statements of account showing moneys received and paid on the client's account. But I think the great deterrent against misappropriations and malpractices on the part of solicitors will be found in the possession of a summary mode of bringing cases of misconduct under the notice of the public Courts, and that the adoption of the suggestions made in reference to the insolvency of solicitors would have the desired effect in speedily lessening the number of those who now annually avail themselves of the "benefit of the Act."

In regard to defaults by fiduciary agents other than solicitors, it would appear that the penalties already applicable would, in the majority of instances, sufficiently guard the public interests, but under the next heading I propose to deal somewhat more particularly with those defaults which trustees acting in bankruptcy matters have been guilty of.

6. In considering what alterations may advantageously be

made in the existing bankruptcy laws to further advance the objects discussed under the previous headings, it will be necessary to restrict remarks to the more immediate object in view. A general dissertation on the amendment of the bankruptcy laws would be of too wide a scope, and to some extent foreign to the subject under discussion. The facilities afforded by the present Bankruptcy Act for enabling debtors generally to relieve themselves from their liabilities have doubtless affected the legal profession as well as the general public. Solicitors advising clients and seeing how easily debts can be "liquidated" would naturally not be slow in case of their own embarrassment to get rid of their debts on the easiest terms. Any amendment therefore of a general character tending to restrict the existing facilities for liquidating and obtaining discharges would *pro tanto* have their natural relation to, and action upon, insolvent members of the legal profession. To attain the desired end considerable alterations in the law will be necessary. If a debtor is to be still allowed to initiate proceedings for arrangement with his creditors, he should, as a preliminary step, be required to show tangible assets available for creditors—"liquidation" with no, or trifling, assets is simply "whitewashing"—it can only benefit the debtor and cannot possibly benefit creditors. Whether the assets to be shown should amount to a certain sum as under the Act of 1849, or whether they should amount to not less than a fixed proportion of the indebtedness, is a matter for consideration. In the next place an arranging debtor should immediately on filing a petition place on record for the information of creditors an account of his property as well as a statement of his liabilities, also a statement of the proposed arrangement he intends to submit for the consideration of his creditors. A meeting of creditors should then be held, the debtor's affairs investigated, and his proposal considered. Restrictions should be placed on the existing system of voting by proxy. Where a debtor's affairs are satisfactory and the creditors entertain his proposals, they should resolve accordingly; but the arrangement should not be complete or binding on dissentient creditors, until personally assented to in writing by a majority in number and four-fifths in value of all the creditors, and approved by the Court. This course would prevent any abuse of proxies at the meeting of creditors, as the matter would subsequently have to be submitted to the creditors personally, and agents would be careful of making improper use of voting powers. Where the creditors decline to entertain a debtor's proposal for arrangement, a simple resolution for bankruptcy should suffice for the purposes of adjudication, when the debtor would become amenable to the provisions of the Act relating to bankrupts. In regard to bankruptcy proper, I think the Court should have some power over the question of discharge, and that restrictions should be placed on the power of voting by proxy on the question of discharging a bankrupt. Any proxy used for the purpose of voting on that question should be given expressly for that purpose, and should state on the face of it whether the agent acting for the creditor is to vote for or against the grant of the discharge. The majority required for assenting to the grant of a discharge should be a majority of the *whole* of the creditors, and not of those who may happen to attend a particular meeting. The Court, even when the statutory majority of creditors assents to the grant of a discharge, should have power to withhold it on specified grounds, especially in case of non-traders.

At present it appears to have no discretionary power if the creditors pass the required resolution. In a recent case a County Court Judge refused the discharge of a bankrupt on the ground that it appeared on the face of the proceedings that his bankruptcy was attributable to rash and hazardous speculation of a flagrant character. This decision was reversed on appeal, and the discharge ordered to be issued, because a resolution had been passed by certain of the creditors to the effect that (in the words of the Act) "the bankruptcy was attributable to circumstances for which the bankrupt could not be justly held responsible," which amounted to their deliberately saying that "a man cannot justly be held responsible for squandering his creditors' money in rash and hazardous speculation."

With reference to the question of debts incurred by fraud or breach of trust, I think the existing provision to which I have previously alluded will suffice. As in the present controversy, I have not seen the point adverted to, I will again call attention to the provision referred to. It is to the effect that an order of discharge shall not release the bankrupt from any debt or liability incurred by any fraud or breach of trust. As such a debt or liability is held to be provable, it follows that a person who has been defrauded by a bankrupt may prove his debt for the amount or value of which he has been defrauded, and receive dividends thereon under the bankruptcy without prejudice to his rights against the defaulting bankrupt. I presume the creditor must not vote on the question of discharge, as thereby he might be waiving any future claim against the bankrupt.

With regard to defaulting trustees in matters of bankruptcy, it has already been pointed out that the existing Act contemplated that all such trustees should provide security for the due performance of the duties of their office. However, the provisions of the Act were rendered to a great extent nugatory by the rules of Court, and the necessity of providing security was not enforced. The consequence has been that creditors have incurred serious losses through absconding and defaulting trustees. Candidates for the office of trustee, if able by means of proxies to appoint themselves to that office, are equally able to resolve that "no security be required from the trustee," or to pass no resolution on the subject. It would be absurd to expect otherwise. The remedy is to require all persons who professionally act as trustees, to provide security *generally* for the due performance of their trust. Such persons might have their names registered in the Court of Bankruptcy on paying a prescribed fee and providing security for a certain amount—in the same manner as official assignees under former Bankruptcy Acts were required to provide security. They would then be eligible for appointment to the office of trustee, and be rendered more amenable to the control and jurisdiction of the Court. The provision of a fixed scale of remuneration for payment of trustees would have a very beneficial effect in preventing many of the existing abuses; and I cannot doubt but that respectable professional trustees would gladly support such a change as, coupled with the requirements as to registration and security, it would relieve them of much of the undue competition for business they have now to contend against on the part of adventurers who have really no claims to the confidence of creditors, and no qualifications for the offices they thrust themselves into by "touting" for proxies.

In reference to the case of solicitors acting for trustees or liquidators in matters of bankruptcy or liquidation, it should not be competent for them to receive moneys due to the estates or companies. Under former Bankruptcy Acts, no receipt for moneys due to a bankrupt's estate was valid, unless signed by the responsible receiver of the estate, namely, the official assignee.

So now no receipt for money due to an estate or company in process of liquidation should be valid, unless signed by the trustee or liquidator. It has happened that where moneys have got into the hands of the solicitor to an estate, instead of into those of the assignee or trustee, years have elapsed before such moneys have been accounted for, or found their way into the pockets of the creditors; in some cases perhaps never. Besides, the trustee or liquidator is personally liable in case of the solicitor's default, and should therefore be protected, as far as possible, by the legislature. Witness a case which recently occurred. A solicitor received a large sum of money—some hundreds of pounds—due to a Company in liquidation. The liquidator knew nothing of this receipt by the solicitor, and consequently did not include it in his accounts. Years afterwards it transpired that the moneys in question had been received by the solicitor. He was brought before the Court, and ordered to pay over the money. Instead of paying he became bankrupt. The parties interested then successfully fixed the unfortunate liquidator personally with the loss occasioned by the solicitor's default, and he had to pay over the amount. If all moneys are bound to be paid to the responsible person—trustee or liquidator—and if the accounts of *all* trustees and liquidators are subject to a periodical *official* audit, a great deal will be done towards securing the due administration of insolvent estates. And an additional protection of the funds of estates might be found in enacting that all moneys not actually required for current expenses in the winding-up should be paid by the trustees into the Bank of England to the credit of the accountant in bankruptcy, and that all dividends should be paid by that officer, as was required in regard to creditors' assignees under the Act of 1861. Trustees would not then, as now, have an interest in delaying dividends by reason of their having the use of the trust moneys for their own purposes; nor would they have in their possession, as they have now, large sums in the shape "of unclaimed dividends," as all such dividends would simply remain in the Bank of England. And as the Comptroller in Bankruptcy has pointed out in his official reports, the interest accruing on the unemployed funds and unclaimed dividends would go far towards defraying the expenses of the Bankruptcy Court, and thus relieve the estates from payment of the fees now charged against them for maintenance of the judicial establishment.

In conclusion, I would remark generally, that while the statistics in regard to defaulting lawyers under the present Bankruptcy Act compare favourably with the state of things which existed under the Act of 1861, still there is reasonable cause for serious attention to the matter on the part of those who have the best interests of an honorable profession at heart. And I do not think that attention can be better directed than to improved action on the part of the Incorporated Law Society, and to the bringing about of such legislative changes as I have briefly alluded to. Attention might also be directed to the consideration of the question whether some more stringent regulations on the part of the Society than now exist in regard to the previous position, character, and *status* of any candidate for admission to the legal profession should not be insisted on. Professional accountants, on their part, would do well to use every endeavour to obtain an Act of Parliament or a Charter of Incorporation for their society, and when obtained to make admission to their ranks dependent on previous character and training, and the possession of a recognized standard of business knowledge and technical attainments, to be tested by duly-qualified examiners.

I can only hope that the foregoing remarks may prove of some practical use, and tend to promote the well-being both of the legal profession and of other fiduciary agents; and will likewise tend to draw particular attention to those defects of the existing Bankruptcy Law, which more especially bear on the questions we have considered, and result in their amendment.

THIRD PRIZE.

MR. WILLIAM H. HAZARD.

THE profession of a solicitor in England, like so many of the institutions under which we live, and which we are sometimes too apt to regard as springing from the nature of things, has a long and instructive history. The exclusive profession of the practice of the law as distinguished from the legislative enunciation of its principles, has, indeed, no clearly defined place in the social systems of antiquity, but has arisen with the growth of modern nations, and its development may be traced throughout the whole of some of their histories. It would, therefore, seem a peculiarly fitting introduction to the considerations which, from the topics of this essay, that we should glance at the events which, from time to time, have been connected with the rise and progress of the solicitor's calling in England.

We have said that the history is a long one, and, indeed, its distinct commencement is found under the early Plantagenets, though traces of a similar calling exercised by the "*cancellarii*," or official scribes of the nobility, are found at a more remote period. We find, however, the "attorney" first legally recognized by the Statute of Westminster II., which was enacted under "England's Justinian"—Edward I.—and among various useful provisions, gave the harassed suitors of that time the privilege they sorely lacked of being relieved from personal attendance on the Courts in their wanderings, if at least they could afford to pay a representative. This personage, however, was at this period generally the advocate, who, owing to the technical development of the primitive law, was becoming a necessity, even where the parties appeared in person. The non-litigious business connected with the transfer of land and management of the feudal Courts which existed in every manor, meantime began, owing to the jealousy which had sprung up of the clergy and their system of Roman or "Canon" Law, to require professed supervisors throughout England, and the scriveners who filled such posts must be taken as the direct predecessors of the modern country solicitor. But in the towns the law was rapidly advancing in its organization of a peculiar profession. Numbers of the nobility, disgusted perhaps with the uncongenial existence of the monasteries, were sending their sons to the Inns which had sprung up for their reception in London, and where regular schools of law were being formed. We have, in our older writers, vivid pictures of the young gentry coming, each with his servant, to one of these inns, where he found a community of 100 or more young men living together and studying, not only law, but with a gymnasium, where music and dancing, and other accomplishments were regularly practised. Still these latter were honestly kept in their place as pastimes, and the Common Law thoroughly occupied the energies of its young votaries. The Common Pleas, its peculiar home, was filled, we read, with crowds of eager students, who flocked thither as early as six o'clock in the morning to patiently await the arrival of the judges, holding, perhaps, meanwhile a "moot" on some vexed point of law. But to keep more within the subject of this essay, we should turn our attention to the closer studies of the young men whom we have seen learning the application of the law in open Court. Fortescue tells us, that the students in the Inns of Chancery were for the most part young men who studied there "the nature of original and judicial writs, which are the very first principles of the law." These Inns of Chancery were so called from their being the peculiar abode of the Clerks of the Chancery, in whose hands the framing of these "original and judicial writs" was from the earliest times; and who, therefore, acted as instructors of the young men who came to these Inns to learn the principles which they saw acted upon in the Courts; and these Clerks of the Chancery were also attorneys, and are described as such by Croke, in his Report on the Court of Chancery in Queen Mary's reign, where he also says :—" The Clarkes were never stinted to any number for two causes—one for and in consideration of bringing up of youth." Hence we see that some of the London attorneys were early filling an important office, and this was long recognized by their being admitted members equally with barristers of the Inns of Court, as well as of the minor Inns of Chancery—though the rising feeling of dislike to them was manifested by several rules from time to time made against their admission to the former, which, however, were very tardily acted upon. Attorneys indeed at this time held a very lucrative and honourable profession both in London and the country, where they developed during the fifteenth century into a well-defined body; and jurisdiction over them was assumed by the municipalities of several towns in the same way as the various trades were regulated, their increasing numbers showing that their practice was very generally sought after. Thus we find that in 1594 all attorneys practising in the Hustings Court of Lyme, except three, were summarily dismissed by the mayor and his brethren from the attorneyships, and very stringent orders as to the conduct of their business were imposed upon the lucky trio who were permitted to remain in their profession (*Roberts'* Social History of the Southern Counties," p. 148), and in 1485, an oft-quoted Act of Parliament reduced the eighty common attorneys who were "stirring up paltry suits" in the Eastern Counties, to six in Norfolk and Suffolk, and two in Norwich. This sage enactment, however, received perhaps unmerited scorn from its origin, and was allowed to remain on our Statute-book a mute protest against the contempt of the "High Court of Parliament," which prevailed in so many similar cases, until 1843.

But not to carry this introductory sketch to too great a length, we may briefly observe that the profession during two or three centuries seems to have steadily declined in position and influence, and though slight indications of progress from time to time appear (as for instance James I.'s Act for the taxation of costs, and the introduction of London agency, which is first traceable under the Commonwealth), yet nearly all the internal energies of attorneys in this direction seem to have been benumbed by the condition of chronic attack and persecution from nearly all classes of society under which they fell during this period. This enduring degradation was in large measure caused (as Mr. Jeaffreson remarks in his "Book about Lawyers") by the ungenerous conduct of the bar, some of whose greatest men were indebted to the very attorneys they were afterwards foremost in sneering at, for their first knowledge of the principles of law : for, as the same gentlemen observes, prior to the rise of special pleaders, attorneys were the most efficient instructors of advocates. Through this influence the London attorneys gradually lost nearly all connection with the centres of legal education, the Inns of Chancery, in which they retained membership, entirely losing their original character and becoming mere blocks of chambers and offices, whose rentals, mostly derived from attorneys, were spent by benchers (who repudiated all association with them) in banquets in the now silent and deserted halls. But it would also seem that a calling like that of attorneys, which stood apart, after their separation from the bar, both from the nobility and the tradesmen or middle classes (for as yet no *upper* middle class could be said to exist), was an easy prey to spiteful witticisms; and that custom soon legalised and turned into bitter earnest the unkind jests of the wit and the dramatist, and afforded such men as Dr. Johnson their only excuse for the causeless antipathy to an attorney which they did not hesitate to evince. The profession, however, though so apparently degenerate, was yet slowly but surely regaining its ground upon the usurped dominion of the bar during the greater part of the last century, and we find many complaints of its gradually increasing importance; and the larger sympathies of the present age have long since freed an honourable body of men from their lengthened surrender to ignominy: for that its endeavours to win a reputation as unsullied as the judicial ermine, are now widely appreciated, the circumstances of this essay afford our best proof.

We have now, we hope, attained a more precise standpoint for the examination of our immediate purpose. We have, as we proposed, glanced at the origin and chequered advance of the solicitor's profession to its present position, but before we discuss the amendments in the profession which it is proposed to make, it seems advisable to devote a few pages to the consideration of its present organization and government—for to possess an accurate diagnosis is an essential preliminary to the course of quasi-medical advice which it is our purpose to offer. It is a singular fact, and well illustrative of the apathy which at once was induced by and assisted the continuance of the increasing virulence with which the profession had so long been regarded, that until 1825 no self-government or organized intercourse of any kind existed within it generally. Such, however, was the case, and, as the Incorporated Law Society's Report for 1850 puts it, "whilst barristers had their halls and libraries, the writers to the signet in Scotland and the attorneys in Dublin their libraries and lecture rooms," the attorneys in England persevered in their primitive individual insulation, submitting indeed to the same laws and admitted to practise by the same authority, but without a single effort towards united self-assertion, and only recognizable thanks to the fiscal motives which prompted the compilation and issue of the annual *Law List*. In 1825, however, a society was at length formed, and it is an instance of our English character of promptitude in pursuing an acknowledged advance, while reluctant to change the existing order of things for an uncertain and untried movement, that its success was speedily complete. By 1827 a large proportion of the £50,000 which it had been resolved to invest in a building, in which the advantages of the kindred bodies above alluded to might be attained, was subscribed, and the well-known Law Institution was erected. A Royal Charter was first granted in 1831, but this was superseded by another in 1845, which abolished the joint-stock character, which, in those days of speculation, it had been necessary to give to the newly-formed society, and firmly established its present constitution (a supplemental Charter in 1872 merely increasing the number of the Council). We may now, therefore, take a survey of the latter. The rules of the society announce that its general purposes are "to promote professional improvement, and to facilitate the acquisition of legal knowledge." Under the Charters of 1845 and 1872, the society is ordered to be governed by a President, Vice-President, and Council to consist of not more than fifty, nor less than twenty ordinary, and ten extraordinary or provincial, members, in whom are vested the sole and entire management of the society. General meetings are to be held annually, and to have the power of making bye-laws, and of electing the President, Vice-President, and Council, and of admitting and expelling members, with reasonable penalties, fines, and amercements in case of breach of the bye-laws; and it is ordered that members rendered incapable of practising by order of any Court of competent jurisdiction for malpractice or other professional misconduct, shall cease to be members. The bye-laws give the council (who are elected for three years) power to suspend members of the society and of their own body, but subject as to the latter to the approval of a special general meeting, and contain other minor provisions.

Such is the constitution of the government not yet half

a century old, which the solicitors of England have imposed upon themselves. Such a decisive step could not but be followed by many and lasting discussions as to its wisdom and advantages, which, indeed, at one time led to a schism in the society's ranks, now happily at an end. The comparative youth of the Law Society prevents its being regarded, by even conservative minds, as the highest attainable goal of perfection, though respect for its wonderfully rapid and admittedly beneficial development should prevent our entertaining for a moment the idea of its supersession and abolition which some of the advanced liberals of the profession still hold. But as we have hinted, improvements are not far to seek in some points of its organization, and it is our duty when such are brought before us to do our best to graft them on to an institution happily young and healthy enough to bear ample pruning and rectification. A lay friend of the profession has urged one of these amendments upon it recently, and has supplemented his advice by inviting the composition of the present essay. The argument he raises is, that as so unhappily large a proportion of solicitors from time to time become bankrupt under somewhat studiously concealed and therefore suspicious circumstances, it would be a measure of justice to the public and the profession that more notoriety should be made to attend such a generally needless abuse of their creditors' and clients' confidence. The discussion which Sir Henry Peek thus started during the early part of this year by his original motion in the House of Commons on the subject, and the letters he afterwards forwarded to the public press, has brought to the front more comprehensive proposals by two gentlemen in the profession for the improvement of its existing discipline. These latter proposals are:—

(1.) That the Law Society should appoint a committee of vigilance, "to consist (we quote from Mr. Munton's letters on the subject), of say, twelve members, half of whom should be selected from the council, and the other half from undoubtedly respectable ordinary members, with the President of the Council as chairman," and that this committee should report up to the general body of the council as such, who should then take action on the result.

(2.) That the society should, as the Registrar of Solicitors "holding an effective and responsible office under the

Crown," enforce discipline generally by, for instance, compelling the punctual renewal of certificates, and taking action on all cases of malpractice "properly brought before it," we may presume by private means.

And the examination of these proposed innovations constitutes the first part of the object which we have placed before us.

But the enormous advance which the general adoption of the comparative system of observation by modern philosophers has produced in every department of science, encourages us to attempt a similar method of inquiry, however imperfectly we may feel that it will be conducted, before we suggest the features that seem most advantageous in these measures of reform.

The legal systems of two foreign countries seem from their intimate connections with our own to afford the most suitable comparisons with that branch of our social government which we are considering. Of these, our nearest neighbour, France, as possessing the longest history and the most instructive contrast in her management of her lawyers, deserves our first notice. We find in France a body of men following the profession of the law, who can trace their origin to the earliest times, and whose constitution seems to have changed but slightly during their long existence. Not to occupy ourselves with the history of the French notaries, which would indeed detain us far too long, let us briefly notice their more prominent charateristics. We are first struck with the primitive rule which prevails, of limiting their numbers by law to ancient and now' inadequate proportions, and which is effected by no new notary being admitted without "la démission du notaire qui se retire en désignant l'aspirant pour son successeur." (*Larousse*, "Dictionnaire du XIX siècle," art. Notaire.) The number of notaries in Paris is thus only 122, and their profession is justly stigmatised as a monopoly by French writers. But though the whole profession is subject to what we should deem an intolerable bureaucracy, and the rules of conduct even to the smallest minutiæ are most vexatious in their restrictions, the French notaries possess some admirable features of self-government. Thus their rules may indeed prohibit "soit par eux-mêmes, soit "indirectement, de se livrer à aucune spéculation de Bourse, ou "opération de commerce, banque, escompte ou courtage; de faire

"des spéculations relatives à l'acquisition et à la revente des im-
"meubles, à la cession des créances, droits successifs, actions
"industrielles, et autres droits incorporels; de placer en leur nom
"personnel des fonds qu'ils auraient reçus, même à la condition
"d'en servir l'intérêt; de se constituer garants ou cautions, à
"quelque titre que ce soit, des prêts qui auraient été faits par leur
"intermédiaire, ou qu'ils auraient été chargés de constater par
"acte public ou privé." (*Larousse ibid.*) But these rules are enforced by an organization that demands our attentive consideration.
The author adds, that, "Les fautes contre la discipline sont pour-
"suivies selon les cas devant *la Chambre de discipline*, ou devant les
"tribunaux civils." And it appears that in each arrondissement
the notaries "se forment en corporation et nomment une chambre
"qui siége au chef-lieu." This chamber elects a chairman and
other officers, and is entrusted with most complete and multifarious powers of supervision of the notaries in its district. "Elle
"veille sur la conduite de chacun, apaise les différends, donne son
"avis sur les honoraires . . . . qui sont fixés par un tarif ap-
"prouvé par le président du tribunal, prononce ou provoque selon
"les cas l'application des mesures de discipline contre ses mem-
"bres." (*Larousse ibid.*) Such a paternal watch have the French
thought it necessary to place over the conduct of their legal
profession, for the *avoués* or practitioners in the Courts are also
subject to a but slightly differing system of coercion, the *Chambre des avoués* being defined as "un conseil composé pour chaque
"siége de membres élus par leurs confrères, ou même de tous les
"avoués du siége quand ils sont audessous de cinq," and exercising nearly the same powers. But, although we cannot admire its
prying inquisition into what *we* have always held strictly private
affairs, yet it forms an acceptable land-mark in connection with the
proposed reforms in our own as yet almost wholly untrammelled
profession. There are one or two other points in this peculiar
system which we must not pass over. As we have seen, the
chambers are elected for three years by the whole body of the
notaries in the arrondissements, and their members are not
allowed to refuse to serve if elected by the chambers as their
officers—the most noteworthy, and probably also unpopular of
whom is the "syndic," who is said to be "la partie poursuivante
"contro les notaires inculpés." The powers of the "*chambre*"
are thus defined by *Clerc* in his "Théorie du Notariat:"—
"Elle peut prononcer suivant la gravité des cas, soit la rappel

"à l'ordre, soit la censure simple par la décision même, soit la
" censure avec réprimande par le président, aux notaires en per-
" sonne dans la chambre assemblée, soit la privation de voix
" délibérative dans l'assemblée générale (the whole body of nota-
" ries), soit l'interdiction de l'entrée de la chambre pendant un
" espace de temps qui ne pourra excéder trois ans pour la
" première fois, et qui pourra s'élever à six ans en cas du récidive ;"
but it cannot decree "suspension ou déstitution" from the
Order, but only advise the higher authorities on these penalties,
for, as the same author says elsewhere, "ses délibérations ne
" sont que de simples actes d'administration," which indeed
it exercises within the above limits without right of appeal.
Another illustration, and we have completed our picture. The
same author says, that "le pouvoir disciplinaire s'étend à tous
" les actes qui pourraient porter atteinte à l'honneur de la
" corporation, ou qui s'écarteraient de la délicatesse, de la
" probité, de la bonne conduite, sans lesquelles un notaire
" n'est plus digne d'estime ni de confiance," but yet, that "le
" pouvoir est en quelque sorte discrétionnaire, mais il ne doit
" jamais dégénerer en une sorte d'inquisition dans la vie
" privée," a curious instance of the French ideas of private life.

We feel that we have exceeded our space in the above description of the French lawyers, but their elaborate regulations
seemed too apposite to our subject not to find a place in our
consideration of it. Let us now pass on to a much briefer
notice of the legal profession of America, before we draw the
comparison we intend between our own proposed reforms, and
the condition of professors of the law abroad. In America, that
land of boasted freedom, the unwearied surveillance of the
French system could not be expected to find a home, and their
control of their lawyers is in entire keeping with the avowed
character of the American politicians. A law of the state of
New York ordains that "every male citizen of the age of
twenty-one years, and properly qualified by his moral conduct,
learning and ability, may become a practitioner in the Courts,"
and there is a similar rule, limited however to "white" male
citizens, in California. Clerkship, however, seems to be required
in some States as a preliminary, and when admitted the Courts
retain a peculiar jurisdiction over their attorneys, which is
called forth by a complaint on oath, and in the exercise of
which a jury is unnecessary. We thus find the Courts striking
attorneys off their rolls for duelling, and in one case for

endeavouring (it is not stated how successfully) to induce another attorney to make a third drunk, on a day when he was to appear in Court as an opponent of the first, and for other unprofessional conduct, as fraud, although not gross enough to be criminally punishable, and the milder penalty of suspension for a limited period is also available in less flagrant cases.

Our consideration of the rules of conduct of the legal profession in France and America has, we hope, assisted in shaping the ideas with which we must now commence the discussion of the proposed reforms in the discipline of solicitors in England. It is a favorable point in the too more definite remedies which we have referred to above, that a certain connection of ideas may be traced between each of them and the corresponding feature of one of the foreign systems we have noticed. The proposal of Mr. Munton, which we placed first, as an original proposition seems well worthy of being carefully weighed, but it gathers additional force from the fact that so similar a system as the "*Chambres de discipline*" form should have been long and universally used in such a powerful and highly civilized nation as France. On the other hand the proposal of the anonymous writer, "S.S.C." in the *Solicitors' Journal*, which we next mentioned, seems in what may be considered an important reform which it upholds, to bear a certain alliance to the American method of procedure against their "defaulting" attorneys, by a process founded on a sworn declaration, but which does not seem to be left in private hands beyond this step. We therefore feel the necessity of carefully examining both the above schemes, and if we are obliged to point out defects in either, we must at the same time feel the weight which the practical adoption of such similar measures by cultivated foreign states adds to them.

We must confess to a decided feeling of dislike on our first view of the French *Chambres*, which indeed the description we have quoted of the degrading surveillance they exercise largely fostered; but our maturer reflections have led us to think that, as we have said, the system relieved from this exaggeration of its legitimate objects, deserves consideration. As has been observed in the published correspondence upon the subject of this essay, " In country districts " (in England), " a man's antecedents are pretty well known, if he has any, and a new comer is the subject of tolerably free criticism and inquiry on the part of those with whom he proposes to compete." Here, then, we see a resemblance (if such it may be called) to the French "*Chambres de discipline*," acknowledged to exist in our own country districts —the whole body of local solicitors, not, perhaps, electing a "committee of vigilance" as in France, but still discussing in the outside world almost as effectually, the good or bad points of "les aspirants" to practice. Unhappily the untrained simplicity of country districts, which admits of the functions of a "*Chambre de discipline*" being exercised in such an *al fresco* manner, is altogether at a loss amid the complex existence of a large town. Here a man may elude the most patient observation of the most inquisitive next door neighbour for months at a time, and all the machinery of public lighting, the police force, stipendiary magistrates, and other artificial methods of self-defence, points to the imperative need felt in such places for more than individual and voluntary restraints on their questionable inhabitants. Why then is not this the case with a profession, which, if happily not now as of old, considered a complete flock of black sheep, still retains a moderate sprinkling of them? The answer has been given by both the gentlemen whose correspondence with the press we have quoted, in their references to "the absence of all autonomy in the profession," and "the utter want of any *esprit de corps* among solicitors." The evil, we see, is admitted; but the remedy must be applied in a different way to that which the public themselves use in lighting their streets and patrolling police through them as a protection from injury. It would be an insult to solicitors to imagine that any such method of suppression of roguery could be enforced among them; but the necessity they are thus reduced to, of becoming their own avengers, has led to the perplexity we find existing as to the means of doing so. This, however, would be assuredly effected by our imitation of the French model in our large towns. Such committees of the more influential solicitors would then be enabled to obtain as exact information as the much to be envied country residents, upon the "antecedents" and general character of every practitioner in their districts who had not, according to their view, the "indefinable something" that may be said to constitute professional respectability. But a too partial view of an innovation must be carefully avoided, and we must, therefore, inquire whether the introduction of a chamber of discipline in every town would encourage the perfection of moral character, which it is the aim of every improvement to advance. Now, an obvious objection occurs to us, that the prying and gossip which are acknowledged to exist in the country, though productive of perhaps but little harm there, would, when organized, and collected by so many powerful bodies throughout England, tend directly to the subversion of that rule which forbids us to bear false witness against our neighbour. The way in which well-educated and responsible men are swayed by the clever insinuations with which an only too common "gift of the gab" can compass its own ends, is so often matter of observation that we should regret to see another series of " local boards," possessing in this case an avowed right of inquisition, established throughout England. And in this point, Mr. Munton's suggested committee differs most advantageously from its French prototypes. His proposal is to have a central committee, formed as we have seen equally from the officers and rank and file of the entire Law Society, and to entrust to this body the powers vested locally in France. The improvement of this scheme upon the mere imitation of the French institution which we have discussed, is easily apparent. In the first place, the number of cases of malpractice, relatively large as it is, yet, is happily not enough so to justify the organization all over England of bodies whose chief, if not only, object would be to direct action against them; while, in the second place, the disadvantages of these local bodies, as their mismanagement and the injuries they might thoughtlessly inflict, are in great measure avoided in such a cosmopolitan body as Mr. Munton suggests, open to discussion from all quarters, and existing in the searching light of London criticism. From such a body the utmost impartiality, tempered with mercy, would be looked for, and its inquiries directed by these feelings would be productive of very general benefit to the profession and the public. But, even in this case, we cannot feel that unqualified success would follow its institution. The anonymous writer, "S.S.C.," whom we have quoted above, has pointed out that " a self-constituted vigilance committee is abnormal in its nature, and very liable to be fitful and uneven in its action." Now such a committee as this, elected as it would be by the whole body of the Law Society and responsible to them, can hardly be called " self-constituted," but we think there is more force in the allegation that it would be abnormal and liable to fitful action.

This certainly seems a probable consequence of its formation for such a special duty as that for which it would be elected. Experience has shown that extraordinary remedies can only succeed when an extraordinary evil has to be combated. Now the percentage of cases of misconduct in the legal profession, though, perhaps, slightly increased of late, can in no way be deemed unusually large, even as compared with that which is found in other callings—indeed, we shall not, as "S.S.C." observes, be able to "look for any marked direct result from whatever measure may be adopted," but only to hope that while evil exists, it may be brought more within the reach of justice than at present. In the existing state of things we should not, so to speak, swear in a body of special constables as though struck with a sudden and causeless panic, but rather calmly prepare to cope with the but too familiar wrongdoers, by strengthening the hands, if you will, but not superseding or supplanting the regular guardians of the peace. We here come upon the gist of the proposal of "S.S.C.," which we have before mentioned. He argues, and justly as we think, that the Law Society with its representative governing body or council are "holding an effective and responsible office under the Crown," and it is to their exercise of that office through the already trained and organized channels that he directs us for the due control of the profession which they represent, and for which they stand, or should stand, responsible. We have said that one of the details of this scheme bears a certain, perhaps rather fanciful, analogy to one of the features in the American procedure which we have described. In that procedure it will be remembered, that the basis of all action taken by the Courts against attorneys is a complaint on oath presumably made by some private person. This method appears similar to that which it is proposed the Law Society should pursue, not perhaps as judge, but as prosecutor and investigator, upon private complaints and information. The radical requirement, of private action in the first instance, is common to both; and this, though sometimes it may not be as prompt in accusation as the collective and irresponsible voice of a committee of vigilance, whether local or centralised, still seems to meet the ideal features of reform more nearly than those suggestions. It is free from the publicity to which the action of any body of men must be more or less subject, and thus has the advantage of at once sparing the innocent accused, or bankrupt solicitor, from the injury which a committee's discussion of his affairs in the first instance would bring on him, while it enables speedier and more inevitable justice to overtake the proved delinquent. But it will be recognised that a central committee of vigilance, such as Mr. Munton has suggested, would also be compelled in many cases to rely on private information for its power of detection of malpractice; and in this point the two schemes we have considered approximate very nearly. Mr. Munton has acknowledged in his published correspondence that he "would not press for the nomination of any members outside the council of the Law Society on his proposed vigilance committee, if their assistance could be usefully dispensed with." We think that it could for the above reason, that the Society has already a very efficient representative body in the shape of its council, perfectly organized (its extraordinary members residing in all parts of the kingdom), and which would rather be placed by such curtailments of its present very varied powers in the condition of "*otium cum dignitate*," which the House of Lords enjoys in our Constitution, than impelled to emulate the active usefulness of the House of Commons. Let it be granted, therefore, that the outside members are absent from the proposed committee, and we then find, not the whole council, but a committee elected from and by it (for an outside election of such a committee would lead to members coming on the council avowedly only for this special duty, and perhaps otherwise unsuited for their office), and differing in this respect alone from the broader, and we venture to think more probably successful, proposal of " S.S.C." Yet we should avoid the suggestion, that the hands of the council are to be in any way tied, or that they should not be at perfect liberty to nominate a select committee at any time. What we wish to point out is, that such a body is, from its very nature, of a temporary character, and that to impart any degree of permanence to it is to negative that character, and to hand over to a limited oligarchy (if the expression may be excused) the powers which at present are wisely vested in the representative governing body or council, itself an imitation in its constitution, of that altogether admirable model, the House of Commons. Let the council, therefore, retain its powers unimpaired, but rather enlarged, to meet the measures of reform it will be expected to undertake, and we may hope to see the latter as effectually carried out as will be possible, while the genius of speculation continues to lead votaries from all classes to ruin, and while clients vie with, in, and tempt weak-hearted solicitors to roguery.

But our task is not yet fully accomplished. We have, indeed, discussed the different organs by which it has been proposed to administer the necessary reforms in discipline, but the powers to be placed in their hands and the processes of reform require our brief mention. The hitherto somewhat neglected subject of these reforms has been sharply agitated of late, and Sir Henry Peek must bear the merit of the success which should attend the vigorous endeavours towards its attainment, which he has been foremost in making. His original ground of accusation has been extended by the correspondence on the subject which we have before referred to, and while it seems now to be admitted that the number of bankrupt solicitors is larger than it ought to or need be, and that some steps should be taken to make such a proceeding a more public and enduring disgrace to the defaulter, it is also alleged that general malpractice demands severer inquisition than it calls forth at present. This is, undoubtedly, the case, and both these evils may well form the subject of immediate and simultaneous reform. We have submitted that this should be effected by charging the Council of the Incorporated Law Society with more vigorous powers than they at present possess, and it remains to see what form such powers could best take. It is evident, as we have said, that information from private sources must constitute the chief ground of action in cases of malpractice—those of bankruptcy being already temporarily public and needing only the inquiry whether they deserve branding or other punishment as frauds. The Council of the Law Society already succeeds in prosecuting numerous cases of professional misconduct thus brought before it, but with others more involved or less flagrant it sometimes seems unable to undertake the tedious and expensive processes of prosecution which are at present necessary. The question thus arises whether the society or its council might not itself be trusted with a certain measure of jurisdiction, and be allowed, like the French Chambers, to inflict mild penalties on its own authority, in cases where punishment, though well deserved, is at present hindered from visiting the offenders. Such a limited authority has long been vested in the College of Physicians, whose President and Censors may admonish, reprimand, or even fine its members in a small sum; and so the College itself, and the Council of the Royal College of Surgeons have power to remove members of their societies. We think, therefore, that a similar addition to the powers of the Law Society, whose responsibility and at least equal capability with the above bodies will be admitted, might safely be made, and that it would prove a simple but effective instrument in its hands in checking and chastising the cases of petty malpractice that so frequently arise.

A striking example of incongruity in the regulations of the profession might also be removed by giving the Law Society its proper authority over the annual publication of the *Law List*. It is a relic of very primitive times to find the Solicitor-General describing this volume as "consisting of two parts, one a book maintained by purely private speculation .... the other a list of solicitors who had taken out on the 1st January duly stamped certificates." In other words, the fiscus is performing for its own immediate advantage what should be of the first consequence to the public, and the rest is left to happy chance. Surely the Registrar of Solicitors ought to have as entire control over the register of that body as the General Medical Council possesses over that of the medical profession, while such an union of the present barbarous divorce would give the Law Society another powerful weapon in their repression of evil-doers—for though bankruptcy may not in every case deserve a stigma, yet a list of the persons annually suspended or struck off the rolls, and, if thought fit, of other severe penalties imposed, would be an insertion of great advantage to the public, but which cannot be fully gained until the Register of Solicitors appears under proper and responsible authority.

It yet remains that we should afford some answer to the important question, through what channel the reforms we have mentioned can be carried out?—and in supplying this we think we shall have reached our limits. The new Bankruptcy Act has been suggested as an available medium for legislation on the subject, but seems rather out of place in connection with it. As has been said, bankruptcy may not of itself deserve further punishment, and if it did the Act would require a separate clause to be inserted for every profession, the members of which are not yet exempted from bankruptcy. But as we have endeavoured to prove, the Law Society is the proper authority to whom the proposed reforms must be entrusted (and how will it so indisputably justify the proud significance of the crest it bears, as by its energetic adoption of effectual measures for the restraint of existing abuses of Justice?) It must therefore itself seek to obtain from Parliament or the Crown an increase of its present powers; but it should first endeavour to identify itself more thoroughly with the profession at whose head it stands, but of whom it unhappily at present barely represents a quarter; though to borrow the language of the Bankruptcy Acts, its members may indeed be said to constitute a clear majority in value, if not in numbers. It would, however, we have no doubt speedily succeed by a little exertion of energy in proselytizing, so to speak, all ranks of the profession, and in gathering them together for united action in the cause of their own and the public good.

We feel that we have now, so far as in us lies, exhausted the important subject of this essay. We are aware that a great deal more effective and more practical might, and doubtless will, be said upon that subject before the discussion upon which our essay is founded has attained its object, or, as we hope is now impossible, has been dropped; but we can honestly acquit ourselves of having left anything undone by which the furtherance of the disinterested motives of its supporters might be assisted, and so must leave what we have written to the kind consideration of our readers, with the feeling that whatever opinion they may form as to its merits, the cause in which it has been undertaken, will, *malgré* our deficiencies, well bear out Spenser's assertion that—

> Everything that is begun with reason
> Will come by ready means unto his end.

CERTIFICATE OF MERIT.

MR. WALTER MILLS.

The slowness with which public opinion matures in England has been so long a national characteristic, that the growth of a formidable scandal in our midst during the past fifteen years, is a matter which, while it excites indignation, can hardly create surprise. During that period, the most important trading community in the world has groaned beneath the operation of a Bankruptcy Law, originally projected with loud praises of the benefits it would confer, but finally condemned, on all hands, as provocative of greater abuses than the system it was designed to remedy or supplant. And, it is to be feared that the new legislation on this subject, now contemplated, will do little or nothing to abate the mischief; and that at the expiration of another decade the same evils will exist in another shape, but perpetrated by a different class of people. It is not our object in the following pages to deal with all the vices of the Bankruptcy Law; we shall address ourselves more especially to the subject of bankrupt solicitors, a topic which has recently attracted much attention in the columns of the public press.

The credit of initiating the inquiry on which we now propose to enter, is due to Sir Henry Peek, who, on the 29th January, 1878, addressed the following inquiry to the Solicitor-General; we extract both question and answer from "Hansard:"—

"Sir Henry Peek asked Mr. Solicitor-General, 'Whether he has considered the desirability (in addition to the other information contained in the annual *Law List*, published by authority) of, in the case of solicitors once, twice, or more times bankrupt, giving the dates of bankruptcy, dividends paid, and the names of assignees of whom detailed particulars might be had; also, in the case of solicitors whose names do not continuously appear in the *Law List*, the reason for omission in occasional years being explained.'"

The Solicitor-General, in reply, said: "He did not think it would be fair to give the names of bankrupt solicitors in the *Law List*, because he did not see why the stigma of bankruptcy should attach to the name of a solicitor for the rest of his life any more than to other classes. The annual *Law List* consisted of two parts. One was a book maintained by purely private speculation, based upon the ordinary sources of information; the other was a list of solicitors who had taken out on the 1st day of January duly stamped certificates. If a solicitor took out his certificate after that date, his name did not appear in the list, which was made up to that date, and that accounted for the names of some solicitors not appearing in the *Law List* from year to year."

For many reasons, chiefly concerning the legal profession itself, it is desirable that the names of all persons duly qualified to act as solicitors, should be published in an easily accessible form from year to year, and that it should not be in the discretion of the solicitor himself whether or not his name shall be so published. But the whole community is affected by the existence of a large body of bankrupt solicitors practising in secret in its midst; and the answer of the Solicitor-General furnishes a clue to the cause of the public indignation, which the prevalence of bankruptcy in the legal profession has evoked. Sir Hardinge Giffard does not see why the stigma of bankruptcy should attach to a solicitor more than to other classes. This argument would be perfectly fair and reasonable if solicitors were on a par with other classes. But a little consideration will show that they are not. The truth is, they are a great public body entrusted by the country with an extensive monopoly, and hence, relied upon individually by private persons as trustworthy state officials. To draw any such comparison as that of the Solicitor-General is therefore wholly unjustifiable.

The word "attorney" originally meant a person who acted for another by virtue of some special or general mandate, and by no means signified what it came at last to mean; it was found, at an early period in the history of English law, that the duty of appearing personally at Westminster to conduct pleadings pressed hard upon suitors. Hence they were allowed by various enactments, commencing in the twentieth year of Henry III., to appoint agents, that is attorneys, to represent them in the Superior Courts of Law. In the fourth year of Henry IV., the number of gentlemen who thus practised as attorneys was very considerable, and in consequence of the free-trade in law then prevalent, abuses had arisen. Hence in 4th Henry IV. cap. 18, it is recited that "sundry damages and mischiefs have ensued * * * by a great number of attorneys ignorant of the law, not learned as heretofore;" and goes on to enact that all attorneys shall be examined by the judges, "and they that be good and virtuous *and of good fame* shall be received." Further on it is enacted that if any such attorney shall be "in default of record or *otherwise*, he shall never after be received to make any suit in any Court of the King." The importance of having reputable, as well as learned attorneys, was thus recognized at an early period. No doubt, if bankruptcy and bubble-company floating had been fashionable at the time the words "default of record or *otherwise*," would have been more precise. It will, however, be observed that in consequence of this enactment, an attorney could have been "taken off the rolls," to use a modern expression, both for gross professional negligence, and also possibly, by virtue of the word "otherwise," if he lost the "good fame" he possessed when admitted to practise. It is suggestive to note in this old statute, that a client is called his attorney's "master;" the number of the profession is also limited, provision being made for filling up vacancies occasioned by death; "and the other attorneys," that is, those who are not sufficiently respectable and learned, "shall be put out by the *discretion* of the judges." In the Act of 2nd George II. c. 23, a penalty of £50 is imposed upon all persons acting as attorneys who are not legally such, and further regulations for examining and admitting them are provided; after 1st December, 1730, no one is to act as an attorney unless he has served a clerkship under articles to an attorney for five years, after which he is to be sworn, admitted, and enrolled. A feeble effort in this direction had been previously made in the reign of James I. (3rd James I. c. 7.) It is to be observed that all these regulations applied solely to attorneys of the Superior Courts at Westminster. In the country and before Courts of Quarter Sessions, &c., anybody could practise as an attorney; this led to public dissatisfaction, and hence the 22nd George II. c. 46 s. 12, which recites that the "mismanagement and unskilfulness of persons employed as solicitors or agents at the sessions * * * and other places of this kingdom, who, having never been regularly bred to the law, and being ignorant of the forms and operations thereof, offenders against the laws of the land have frequently escaped with impunity." It is then provided that after the 29th September, 1749, "no person whatsoever shall act as a solicitor, attorney, or agent * * * unless such person shall have been heretofore admitted an attorney of one of His Majesty's Courts of Record at Westminster, or unless such person shall hereafter be admitted an attorney and enrolled." These Acts have subsequently been consolidated and amended; a monopoly in favour of duly admitted and enrolled attorneys and solicitors has now been established; and they are now, in legal language, "Officers of the Courts of Law."

The foregoing facts conclusively show that the special legal agent popularly known by the name "solicitor," is not on a par with "other classes," and should not be compared with them, as was most improperly done by the Solicitor-General. Originally created with the view of conducting pleadings in the Law Courts, the order of solicitors has gradually attracted to itself, by virtue of the confidence which the public invariably reposes in duly-accredited state officials, a vast amount of collateral business, all of which is entrusted to its members in consequence of their *status* and respectability. The history of the law, which creates and regulates them, conclusively shows : 1st, that they are necessary to the proper administration of justice; 2nd, that free trade in law is detrimental to the interests of the community; 3rd, that the establishment of a monopoly in favour of properly qualified individuals is the only way by which society can be efficiently served and protected. It follows that solicitors are not, and ought not to be, comparable with ordinary traders, in seeking to remedy abuses which may exist in the profession. As an illustration of this principle, we find that by the 28th George II. c. 13 s. 23, it is provided that where solicitors, attorneys, or persons acting or pretending to act as such, become insolvent, a discharge under the Insolvency Acts shall not liberate them from debts with "which he or they shall stand charged for any money or other effects recovered or received for the use of any person or persons, and by any solicitor, attorney, &c., embezzled, concealed, or converted to his or their own use." This Act recognizes and enforces the fiduciary relationship existing between solicitor and client. Unfortunately, this relationship has been either ignored or overlooked by the Bankruptcy Act, 1869, under the provisions of which a solicitor is enabled to rid himself of liabilities to his clients as soon as he has succeeded in dissipating their property.

Sir Henry Peek's question, and the Solicitor-General's reply, necessarily attracted much public comment, and a correspondence on the subject took place in the columns of several newspapers. Mr. F. K. Munton, in a letter which was printed in the *Echo*, on the 15th February, asserts that, having kept a private register of bankrupt solicitors, since 1861, the result is an appalling catalogue of defaulters. In another letter on 16th March, to the *Solicitors' Journal*, he gives the number of them as nearly 850. It seems that of these, 350 reside in London, and the remainder in the provinces. Sir Henry Peek, in a letter which appeared on the same day and in the same journal, gives a more particular analysis ; taking all the solicitors in the *Law List* whose names commence with the letter *D*, of which there are 155, he finds that eleven of them, or seven per cent., have become once or oftener bankrupt, and this does not disclose the total number of members of the profession whose names begin with *D* who have become insolvent, since many such, for reasons best known to themselves, omit to take out their annual certificate in time to ensure insertion of their names in the List.

It could not be supposed that apologists for the defaulters would not be forthcoming ; one such made his appearance under the cloak of the initials "S.S.C." He appears to look upon Sir Henry Peek as his natural foe, for he naïvely writes, "*Fas est et ab hoste doceri*," and asserts that it is absurd to expect all solicitors to be "ideal," the meaning of which we presume is that when a solicitor finds he is not able to obtain a living as such, he is justified in dabbling in extraneous speculations, and, at the same time, in reserving the respectability which the *status* of his profession confers as a resource in case his bubbles collapse. Evidently the "ideal" solicitor of " S.S.C." is a sort of free-lance enveloped in an impenetrable cloak of "respectability," who is at liberty to sally forth from his stronghold at his own caprice, certain of safe quarters on his return, should any mishap have overtaken him. After enunciating this sublime theory, " S.S.C." proposes that, in cases of bankruptcy, the Incorporated Law Society should inquire into the circumstances attending a solicitor's insolvency, and hang up a list of names somewhere, distinguishing the unfortunate from the fraudulent.

The objection to this proposal is that it is perfectly impracticable; it would be utterly idle to attempt to find out the circumstances attending a solicitor's bankruptcy, without holding a public inquiry and giving notice of it to every one of the creditors. Some of these perhaps might attend if the place of meeting were convenient and their expenses paid; but in all probability the greater part of them would keep away, and means would be adopted to silence such hostile ones as might be disposed to come. Add to all which, the task of conducting such inquiries would be far beyond the powers of any such body as the Incorporated Law Society, even supposing it were lawful to hold them. We will, however, for argument's sake, suppose that one such investigation has been held, and, as a result, some solicitor's name is duly posted up in the list of rogues. Having nothing in the world to lose, and the chance of gaining something by a successful verdict, the defaulter would, unquestionably, bring an action for libel, to defend which would necessitate the reopening of the previous inquiry, at enormous expense, and very probably with a diametrically different conclusion. These objections will apply with equal force to the working of a vigilance committee of the society; this committee would experience insuperable difficulty in collecting evidence on which dependence could be placed. Take the case of a bankrupt country solicitor; putting jealousy on one side, inasmuch as statistics show that one in twenty actually becomes insolvent, and probably one in ten is in a highly critical condition, many of those who were called upon to give a character to their townsman would possess that fellow feeling which produces such kindly results. Finally, the names of the outcasts would not be accessible to the public, or at any rate not so without a special inquiry at the place of publication, and hence little general benefit would ensue. We do not therefore anticipate any permanent improvement in the existing state of things, unless a remedy of a very different nature be applied.

In addition to the scandals arising from solicitors becoming bankrupt, it has been pointed out that other evils equally serious arise from the professional malpractices of those who, in the words of Mr. F. K. Munton, are "always on the verge of insolvency, and who adopt all kinds of tricks and devices so embarrassing to those who have to deal with them." From such practitioners, the process of obtaining a client's moneys or securities is tedious and inefficient, whereas, it being the law that he shall give them, upon demand, providing his proper bill of costs is paid, there should be a means of bringing him speedily to account. It is also perfectly well known that some solicitors cannot be got to send in a bill at all until extreme measures are resorted to. One such recently came under our notice ; he had been employed to dispose of some mortgaged property, which he did, and in reply to repeated applications for an account from the mortgagor, finally sent a short note informing him that the bill of costs came to more than the equity of redemption realised. This same gentleman, some months previously, acted as solicitor to a limited company, formed to purchase a mine which did not exist ; he allowed his name to be attached to a prospectus of the company, in which it was stated that a dividend of ten per cent. per annum had been guaranteed by Members of Parliament, whose names were given. On the faith of these representations, money was subscribed, but when the company went into liquidation, it turned out that the statement as to the guarantee was wholly without foundation. Nevertheless, this gentleman still continues to act as "Solicitor and Commissioner to administer oaths in Her Majesty's High Court of Justice" as per the plate on his door. It has been pointed out that the practice, where a solicitor detains moneys and deeds is this :—First he is called upon by summons to deliver his bills and accounts ; if he disregards the order made on this summons, he may be attached for contempt, but he may purge his contempt by delivering his bills and accounts, still detaining the property until the bills are taxed. We are within the mark in asserting that by the judicious employment of professional artifices a solicitor may keep his client without an account for three months at the least. Meanwhile he may be inflicting the most serious injury on his client, while employing the funds thus immorally (not illegally) withheld, at his own discretion. There is, it is true, another method of proceeding by applying for an order to answer matters on affidavits, but this being of a quasi-criminal form, has been discountenanced by the Court, except where it is used as a means of actually removing a solicitor from the rolls. For these abuses it is easy to suggest a remedy at once cheap, speedy, and effectual. A solicitor is at law bound to keep his accounts constantly ready for production to his client, hence a summons to produce his accounts should be made returnable on the following day ; on the hearing of this summons, unless the accounts were produced, the solicitor should be called upon to state the probable amount of his bill; this sum should be paid into Court to abide taxation, and an order be made upon the solicitor to deliver up any deeds, &c., *instanter*, or in the case of money, to pay over the balance. Disobedience to this order should amount not only to contempt, but to a conversion of the property. There are few solicitors who would care to undergo imprisonment, in addition to running the risk of an action for damages, which, doubtless, in most cases would be exemplary.

In connection with this difficulty of obtaining moneys from certain solicitors, we would point out a similar abuse, but a graver one since it is perpetrated by the immediate officers of the law. We refer to the delays and difficulties interposed by under-sheriffs in the way of obtaining the fruits of an execution. In cases where the amount levied exceeds £50, they are entitled to retain it for a fortnight, but by a law of their own making, it is next to impossible to get *any* sum from them in less than a month, that is unless a "rule" be resorted to, which is rarely done since it is looked upon as a hostile proceeding. Trustees to bankrupts, detaining moneys of the estate in their hands, are liable to pay twenty per cent. interest where it exceeds a certain sum, and it is suggested that the movements of under-sheriffs would be greatly accelerated were a like regulation to apply to them.

It was pointed out by Mr. Munton, in a letter which appeared in the *Solicitors' Journal*, of 13th April, 1878, that "perhaps many of the people who figure in the *London Gazette* as bankrupt solicitors, are not really solicitors; * * there are names in the *London Directory* under the head of solicitors that can neither be found in the *Law List* nor on the Law Society's manuscript roll." This little matter I commend to the notice of the authorities. In the *Daily Telegraph*, of 25th September, appears an account of the doings of one of this fraternity.

"BOW-STREET.—ALLEGED FRAUD AND FORGERY.—*Edward Laurence Levy*, of 28, Leicester-square, was charged on remand, before Mr. Flowers, with having converted to his own use a valuable security for £111 10s. 9d., that had been entrusted to him by one Jules Rivière and another. Mr. St. John Wontner prosecuted on behalf of the Treasury; Mr. George Lewis, Jun., appeared for the prisoner. In opening the case Mr. Wontner said the specific charge upon which the prisoner was arrested was one of having misappropriated a draft for £111 odd, which had been entrusted to him as an agent by Messrs. Rivière and Hawkes, music publishers, of 28, Leicester-square. The prosecution had been instituted by the Home Secretary, as, in addition to that charge, there would be several others of a more serious character—charges of forgery—preferred against the accused. The prisoner was some years since a solicitor, and latterly he had been assisting to carry on the business of a solicitor, under the style of Fisher & Co. Mr. Rivière became acquainted with the prisoner, and, believing him to be a solicitor, entrusted him with business, and subsequently gave him debts to collect. They had perfect faith in Mr. Levy, and, as he always told them he had been unable to get any of these moneys in, the firm allowed matters to go on until one day they themselves applied to a person who, they believed, owed them an account, and they then found that the amount had been paid."

And then of course follows a list of the defalcations of Mr. Levy, otherwise Fisher & Co. The case is a typical one; a man sees "Fisher & Co., Solicitors," on a brass plate for a certain number of months or years, necessarily supposes the firm to be trustworthy professional men, and when he has debts to collect places the matter in their hands. And eventually he is defrauded. But what the public are entitled to ask is why has Levy been allowed to practise as a solicitor at all? Are there no penalties provided in cases where persons act as solicitors who are not so? Whose business is it to weed out the sham from the real solicitors? Surely *this* might be a duty which the Incorporated Law Society could undertake. It is perfectly well known in the profession that numbers of men practise as solicitors either in their own name or in that of another; yet nothing whatever is done to abate the mischief. About ten years ago an "Association" for the protection of the commercial world was launched by one of these, whom we will call Mr. Dash. This gentleman being deeply in debt announced himself to the world as Blank & Co. One day he received a communication, addressed to him as Blank, from a resident in the country, desiring him to apply for payment to Mr. Dash "who carries on business in the same building as your association." It is unnecessary to add that several fruitless applications for the money were made by Blank & Co., Solicitors, to Mr. Dash, and a bill of costs accumulated in due course. Now this sort of thing continued for a long time, and came to an end without any official notice of Blank & Co.'s doings being taken by the accredited representatives of the legal profession. *Ex uno disce omnes*; doubtless there are many successors of Mr. Dash actively engaged in fleecing their victims, for the assumption of the name "solicitor" by one who is not so, can be with no other object than that of fraud. But who, may we ask, is the Fisher, of Fisher & Co., alias Levy? Is there such a solicitor as Fisher, who, for a consideration, allows Levy to use his name? This question brings to mind another scandalous professional mischief, unhappily too prevalent. In London more particularly there are many establishments, some doing a very considerable business, carried on in the name of a solicitor who actually does nothing but sell the use of his name to irresponsible agents. In the event of anything going wrong which entails the appearance of the solicitor to answer for deeds done in his name in a Court of Justice, the appeal *ad misericordiam*, that the act was perpetrated by his clerk without his knowledge, is made and prevents removal from the rolls. And will it be credited that the Courts themselves tolerate or ignore these malpractices? Yet that they do must be evident to anybody who has visited the Judge's Chambers and noticed the class of men who appear there as "the defendant, his solicitor, or agent" to answer summonses. It is of course essential that many matters of practice should be capable of being conducted by a solicitor's clerk, but it is stretching the rights of suitors too far to permit persons who are neither solicitors, nor in their employ, to act officially in suits.

In the course of the correspondence in the *Solicitors' Journal* on this subject, one writer remarks:—"What one solicitor needs to know about any other, is not merely whether he has kept out of the Bankruptcy Court, but whether he fights fair, and whether his word may be relied on." Doubtless this observation is perfectly accurate; yet, to some extent, indeed in a very great measure, the solvency of a solicitor is a criterion of fair-fighting. Where a solicitor becomes bankrupt in consequence of his embarking in trade speculations, it is evident he does not look to his profession as a means of livelihood, and hence will be guided in his professional duties not by the delicate conscience and scrupulous etiquette of a true lawyer, but by the consideration whether sharp practice and unfair behaviour will or will not *pay* better in the particular matter he may have in hand. When the bankruptcy is caused by the improper use of client's money, it must be evident that he who is unscrupulous in his dealings with those who pay and trust him, cannot be relied on between party and party. It has been very properly observed that in consequence of the stringent ruling of the Courts of Law on the liabilities of partners, it sometimes happens that one who, as regards his own affairs, is perfectly solvent, is liable to become bankrupt by his partner's folly. No doubt this occasionally happens, and it in no way affects the validity of our argument that bankruptcy in solicitors should set all men on their guard in dealing with them; for let us suppose the firm of Brown and Jones became bankrupt through the default of Jones. Brown's estate pays 20s. in the pound, that of Jones *nil*. The partnership estate pays 6d. in the pound. If, in the face of these facts, Brown continues his partnership with Jones, will it not argue the most unscrupulous recklessness, and justify any one in being suspicious of the firm? It would be perfectly easy, in dealing with bankrupt partnerships, to provide that none of the professional disabilities entailed upon a solicitor by bankruptcy should apply to those members of a firm whose separate estates were sufficient to discharge the claims upon them. Apropos of these partnerships, what is the meaning of the word "Co.," which one sees now and then at the end of a legal firm? It used not to be considered professional to have a partner of whose name one is ashamed, or which would not add to one's reputation. Yet of late years, the "Co." has become more and more prevalent with solicitors. Without wishing to make a universal condemnation of all such firms, we will go the length of asserting this, that it is best to avoid them, or at least to institute some inquiries before dealing with them.

Again, bankruptcy in the case of a solicitor is discreditable and infamising for the same reason that it is so in the case of any other person, viz., that, as a rule, it is the resort of unprincipled people. Doubtless, individual instances now and then occur in which insolvency is due to pure misfortune, but in most cases it is nothing of the sort. The bankrupt, as a rule, looks upon "the Court" and "going through it" as a means of making money. He makes his arrangements and bides his time in precisely the same way that he watches the course of the markets. If the truth of this assertion is doubted, it may be substantiated by the statistics published by the Comptroller in Bankruptcy. These show that as the working of a Bankruptcy Act gets to be understood, and debtors become familiar with artifices designed for their benefit, so dividends decrease. During the first year or two of the existence of the present law, it was currently supposed that in order to "go through the

Court," at least ten shillings in the pound must be paid; hence a very appreciable number of such dividends during the period. Latterly, however, this idea has been exploded; consequently the number of those paying ten shillings in the pound has declined from 482 in 1870 to 249 in 1875; at the same time, those who pay less than a shilling in the pound, have risen from 94 in 1870 to 541 in 1875. These are plain facts; they expose the facilities for fraud which the Bankruptcy Law affords, and when we find a solicitor taking the benefit of such an enactment, we are entitled to ask very seriously, "What manner of man is he?"

Various suggestions have been made as to the best way of grappling with and preventing the evils enumerated in the foregoing pages, and with these propositions we have now to deal. But, before doing so, we would observe that a competent tribunal for enforcing discipline among solicitors, to say nothing of morals, does not exist. Theoretically, no doubt, there is such a body, but in practice it falls far short of what the public and the profession may fairly demand. Hampered by the strict rules of evidence, and bound by precedent, a Court of Law is not suited to enforcing professional etiquette, or to defining what is or is not conduct worthy of a member of a liberal profession; for both these matters fluctuate from year to year, and therefore are incapable of circumscription within strict legal definitions. And many objections may be made to the Incorporated Law Society acting as registrar of solicitors, dealing with these subjects. It should be recognized, we venture to think, that the profession of the law embraces, at law, both solicitors and barristers. Technically, we think that at present this is not so. A solicitor is a paid agent—of a very special sort, it is true,—but the exigencies of society have long required him to be much more than this; and the time has come when the profession of the law, whether as a solicitor or as a barrister, should be looked upon as a whole, and not as consisting of two heterogeneous parts. A bill for regulating the discipline of practitioners at the Bar has already been before Parliament; it entrusts the enforcement of that discipline to a tribunal of the competence of which there can be no dispute. With proper modifications, to the same body of men should be committed the regulation of those who practise as solicitors: it should be their duty to remove from the rolls the name of any solicitor who has been guilty of grossly unprofessional conduct; and what this may amount to we would leave to them to decide. At the same time, the Incorporated Law Society might imitate, with advantage both to itself and the community, the course of action pursued by the Apothecaries' Company with regard to unauthorized medical practitioners. That corporation constantly prosecutes unlicensed medical men; is it asking too much to request the Incorporated Law Society to do the same as regards irregular legal practitioners? In this way, while authorized members of both branches of the legal profession would be amenable to the jurisdiction of a tribunal, the impartiality and independence of which would remove suspicion from its decisions, those who lacked due authority to practise would find their movements watched, and their doings punished, by a body of men whose direct interest it is to do so.

We have already shown that it concerns the public as well as the profession, to be able to know whether a solicitor has been bankrupt. Sir Henry Peek's proposal, or rather suggestion, that this information should be furnished in the *Law List*, is open to many objections. First, the public do not read the *Law List*, many of them being unaware of its existence; next, there are many worthless and unprincipled solicitors who have never been bankrupt, and these would flourish more vigorously than ever in the list of solvent men. As a logical sequence of the arguments already put forth, removal from the ranks of the profession should be peremptory in all cases where a solicitor is bankrupt, and he should not be reinstated until his debts have been paid in full. Such a proviso may seem harsh, yet it should be remembered that a solicitor is a client's *alter ego*, as it were, and for such a man to mismanage his own affairs furnishes a positive proof that he is unfit to conduct those of other people. Individual hardship would, no doubt, sometimes arise under the operation of such a rule, as it always will in matters with which human intelligence has to deal, but the community at large would gain immensely, and it is their welfare alone that legislators should look at. It is, no doubt, hard to lose a seat in Parliament, which has entailed an outlay of thousands of pounds, or membership of a Town Council, by misfortune in trade resulting in bankruptcy, yet the public welfare demands that such should be the law, and we see no reason why solicitors should not be brought under a similar enactment. Yet it will be urged that hard cases make bad law: those who would not even attach a "stigma" to a bankrupt solicitor will not, *à fortiori*, prevent him from practising. Yet the reason why privileges are conferred upon him, and admission to the calling he follows hedged about with restrictions is, that wherever there is a solicitor there should also be a gentleman, in whom a client may confide without previously investigating his antecedents. It seems absurd that, in a community which will not allow a man who, at any period in his life, has been convicted of stealing even a postage stamp, to sell beer, a solicitor may rob with impunity under the protection of bankruptcy laws, and return with fresh vigour to the field of his depredations. We write advisedly: for bankruptcy, in a solicitor, arising solely from his professional duties, would be robbery at law, if there were any means of getting at the evidence; and, when a solicitor becomes bankrupt from causes extraneous to his profession, it is clear he cannot live by it, and hence should be excluded from it.

Yet it is not always advisable to apply a drastic remedy where gentler means may prevent a recurrence of the disorder, and excessive severity, by arousing sympathy, frequently excites commiseration where none is deserved. We would not, therefore, go the length of striking a bankrupt solicitor off the rolls. As a tentative measure other means of correction may be adopted, which, if found inadequate, can be supplemented, after due trial, by stronger ones. We suggest the same course as that pursued when medical men are found guilty of infamous professional conduct. The immediate effect in their case is to prevent them from suing for their fees, not from practising. We therefore propose that whenever a solicitor becomes bankrupt, he should be disqualified from bringing any action to recover his professional charges until he had received a certificate that his debts had been paid in full. During this period his name should also be omitted from the *Law List*. The result of this provision would be that those solicitors who now neglect to take out their certificates in time to obtain insertion of their names in that List would, in future, be specially careful that their names should appear. At the same time the public would be supplied with an incentive to consult the *Law List*, which is wanting at present. In every case where an action of importance is brought, a cheque on account of costs is asked for at an early stage: we may be sure a client would not write that cheque without looking at a *Law List*. If he found his solicitor's name there, he would pay his money with renewed confidence; if he did not, he would be in a position to withdraw in time, or to demand explanations before becoming further involved. As regards the solicitor himself, he would either honourably discharge his past debts by his professional exertions, or if his practice did not warrant him in supposing such a contingency possible, would quit it for some other calling. Either of these courses would be open to him, and neither infringes on the duty he owes to his fellow-man.

It is an old saying that men cannot be made virtuous by Act of Parliament; it may also be affirmed that they cannot be made gentlemen by such means. A cunning youth may be sent into a lawyer's office, and emerge in due course a solicitor, with sufficient knowledge of the letter of the law to enable him to avoid its clutches. To such an one it is idle to talk of professional etiquette, which he does not understand, and practises as little as possible. From the ranks of this class defaulting solicitors are recruited; it cannot be a matter of indifference to the legislature that such people exist, and prey upon society, nor, when the evil is patent, should there be any hesitation in applying a remedy.

CERTIFICATE OF MERIT.

MR. JAMES RIGBY SMITH.

On the 29th January, 1878, Sir Henry Peek asked the Solicitor-General in the House of Commons, "Whether he has considered the desirability (in addition to the other information contained in the annual *Law List*, published by authority) of, in the case of solicitors once, twice, or more times bankrupt, giving the dates of bankruptcy, dividends paid, and the names of assignees of whom detailed particulars might be had; also in the case of solicitors whose names do not continuously appear in the *Law List*, the reason for omission being explained." The Solicitor-General said in reply, that "he did not think it would be fair to give the names of bankrupt solicitors in the *Law List*, because he did not see why the stigma of bankruptcy should attach to the name of a solicitor for the rest of his life, any more than to other classes."

This episode gave rise to a discussion in the pages of the *Solicitors' Journal* and the *Echo*, which brought to light the following facts. Since the passing of the Bankruptcy Act of 1861, which, for the first time, enabled professional men to avail themselves of the bankruptcy laws, until the end of 1876, 371 London, and 452 country solicitors became bankrupt. (Mr. Francis K. Munton in *Solicitors' Journal* of 16th March, 1878.) As a test investigation, Sir Henry Peek had the published antecedents of a certain number of solicitors inquired into with the following result. Of the 155 names under the letter "*D*" in the *Law List* of 1878, eleven names, or seven per cent., were found to have figured discreditably in the *Gazette*. Under the letter "*W*," however, according to the *Solicitors' Journal*, only three per cent. have failed. Mr. Munton draws the general conclusion that one solicitor out of twenty becomes bankrupt. The same gentleman affirms that, out of the 371 London defaulters, forty-nine have failed twice; eight, three times; three, four times; and one has passed through the Court on five separate occasions.

All the writers in this discussion agree that the state of things disclosed is very serious, both for the profession and the public. The remedies suggested are of two kinds: the provision by authority of a more perfect and accessible record of the fact of bankruptcy; and, disciplinary action from within the body of solicitors. The members of the profession who have taken part in the discussion, for the most part, strongly object to the former of these modes of action, and are of opinion that the difficulty can be met by judiciously chosen proceedings of the latter kind. One writer (*Solicitors' Journal*, 30th March, 1878) suggests: "The proper and the only fitting mode of dealing with the matter is one of discipline, and the proper dispenser of that discipline is, in my opinion, the Incorporated Law Society in its capacity of registrar of solicitors." Mr. Munton (*Solicitors' Journal*, 30th March, 1878) stated, that: "It is my intention to move at the next annual meeting of the Incorporated Law Society, for the appointment of a Vigilance Committee to be charged with the special duty of inquiring into malpractices and defalcations; and, as to bankruptcy, I propose that, in the absence of reasonable explanation (*i.e.*, it should be incumbent on a bankrupt solicitor, having regard to his position of trust, to establish a case of *primâ facie* misfortune), the Council should be empowered to oppose the renewal of certificates."

There is, however, a preliminary reason of great force for doubting the efficacy of any action of this kind. The interests to be guarded are those of clients and the public; any one who supposes that these interests would be in safe keeping in the hands of representatives of the class whose members imperil them, must have very little knowledge of human nature or of the perverse kind of *esprit de corps*, that is found whenever separate interests create a distinct class. The report of the Royal Commission of inquiry into the Stock Exchange, acquaints us with the results of an experiment of an analogous kind. The Committee of the Stock Exchange already exercise the kind of disciplinary power, which, entrusted to the Incorporated Law Society, would, on the hypothesis under notice, solve the difficulty arising from the large number of defaulting solicitors now in practice. *The Times*, of 17th August, 1878, makes the following remarks on the conduct of the Stock Exchange Committee : "It would appear that the Committee have been unduly lax in the matter of the admission of defaulters. Out of 105 who obtained re-admission, 78 had been condemned to exclusion for indiscretion and the absence of reasonable caution, and this leniency can scarcely be defended. The Committee have also been slow in their oversight of the conduct of members, who have been content to do business with needy speculators, who have been led on to insolvency and ruin. One of their rules condemns such conduct, but it has not been vigilantly applied. Closely connected with this tenderness is the *esprit de corps*, which has brought about the unwritten rule, that the name of a defaulter on the Stock Exchange is never communicated to the outside world, so that the unguarded client may be allowed to continue dealing with an acknowledged insolvent without knowing it. We cannot but think that, now that public attention has been drawn to these matters, a little wholesome rigour will be adopted by the Committee." Should the objection against the alternative or publicity mode of action prove insuperable, some kind of disciplinary action from within the body of solicitors would be better than nothing; but only a mind of a very sanguine order, or a mind inspired by the dread of the alternative mode of proceeding, could entertain any hope of a successful treatment of the evil by any method of this kind. A council acting on behalf of the general body of solicitors might, however, very usefully conduct the inquiries necessary to qualify the public record, should an improved kind of record be adopted. in the interests of comparatively innocent insolvents. In this capacity they would be legitimately acting in the interests of members of their own class, and the ordinary motives to zeal and efficiency would not be wanting.

It remains to consider the objections to the alternative mode of action. The ground of objection taken by the Solicitor-General to the proposal of Sir Henry Peek raises two issues, one of them a very wide one. It may be urged in answer to the Solicitor-General that there are special reasons that do not apply to other classes, why the public fact of a solicitor's bankruptcy should not be allowed to fade from public knowledge, or it may be asserted that the mantle of oblivion that covers the antecedents of bankrupt solicitors, as well as of bankrupts of other classes, is altogether a public evil. On the narrower question it may be said that the interests entrusted to a solicitor are of a more intimate and vital kind than those involved in ordinary commercial relations, and further, insolvency in the case of a solicitor is a deeper stain on character than in the case of a trader, because the solicitor's risk in his professional transactions is not so great; hence there is a double reason for a different and more stringent treatment. It might, however, be difficult to show that this difference is serious enough to justify the proposal of Sir Henry Peek, and should the wider question be determined in a sense unfavourable to the claim set up on behalf of "other classes," it will be unnecessary to make the attempt.

Before grappling with the general question, whether it is a good thing that the public fact of a man's insolvency should be allowed to slide into oblivion, to the great advantage of the insolvent, and to the probable prejudice of persons who have future dealings with him, a narrower question framed on the model of the Solicitor-General's answer may very well be put, namely, why should bankrupts in London enjoy a greater immunity in this respect than provincial bankrupts, whose antecedents, it is admitted, are perfectly well known? If it is really a good thing that the fact of previous insolvency should be hidden away from the insolvent's future connection, some serious steps might be taken artificially to extend this benefit to the provinces, where at present the tenacity of the provincial memory, and the communicativeness of the provincial mind inflict so cruel a wrong upon the unfortunate provincial bankrupt. Clearly, if the conditions prevailing in London are fair and beneficial, those prevailing in the provinces are unfair and hurtful: the *status quo* is obviously unjust, either to the London client, or to the provincial practitioner. This comparison between town and country shows how the immunity enjoyed by town bankrupts arises; it is pure accident, depending upon the density and migratoriness of population. This fact is important, because it gets rid of the objection that applies to all innovation. The question really is, shall an improvement in the public record of a public fact be made to neutralize certain recent changes in the conditions, which have caused the old form of record to be of little value. The answer to this question depends upon whether the greater or the less publicity is most favourable to the interests of the community. The more perfect record guards intending clients from the risk of unknowingly committing their interests to the care of a defaulting solicitor, and the trader from giving credit to buyers who have not always paid twenty shillings in the pound. On the other hand, the less perfect record gives an insolvent solicitor or trader more chance of repairing an error or misfortune in his professional career. The former diminishes the risk to innocent clients and traders, the latter removes difficulties from the way of the insolvent. It is impossible to pay regard to one of these interests without ignoring the other; the gain of the one and the loss of the other, are only two aspects of the same fact. The clients are the more numerous, and therefore their interest would seem more nearly identical with the public welfare; the clients, moreover, have no presumption in their disfavour, which to some extent the insolvent has.

A somewhat analogous question, namely, which set of interests has the greater claim on the regard of the public authority, admits of a more obvious answer. Society has already conferred a great obligation on the bankrupt by stepping in between him and his creditors, and shielding him from all further pursuit and annoyance, securing, in fact, his interest at the expense of his neighbours. In the new question that then arises, the neighbours, and not the insolvent seem, in justice, to have the first claim to regard.

The most cogent reason in favour of the more perfect record is that society, by bankruptcy legislation, has created the danger to the innocent client or trader, and is therefore bound to furnish a corresponding safeguard. Were the bankrupt not delivered from his former creditors, he would be unable to secure fresh victims to his business ineptitude or his fraudulent operations. The least thing the law can do, in discharge of the responsibility it assumes in starting the insolvent afresh on his doubtful career, is to provide an ample and easily accessible record of its action in the matter.

This general conclusion is not supported by any writer in the discussion under review. Sir Henry Peek says: "As regards bankruptcy, I maintain that the position of professional men and men of business are so widely different, that exactly the same treatment should not be applied." On the basis of this admission, the question is very difficult to argue; it would be necessary to show in fact that the difference in the proposed treatment did not more than cover the difference of culpability in the two classes. On the other hand, the plea for an easily accessible general record admits of straightforward and powerful logical support. It is not, be it remembered, a question between a record and no record, but between a record easy and one difficult to consult. The investigations made, at the instance of Sir Henry Peek, show that the present record is available for any one who can go to the trouble or expense of consulting it.

Mr. Munton is not inclined to go so far as Sir Henry Peek; he admits "few can gainsay the answer of the Solicitor-General that it would be going too far to publicly note every lawyer's bankruptcy in the *Law List* by a distinctive mark," but he would "not be sorry to see ample publicity given to all failures traceable to speculation." This seems to be a more unworkable line of distinction than Sir Henry Peek's. If once the principle of a "proper record" (in Mr. Munton's own phrase) is given up, no hope of any adequate remedy remains. In the case of trades and most professions, the great difficulty would be to form the register, but in the case of solicitors this already exists in the *Law List*, it only remains to add the distinctive marks. There is difference enough between the cases of solicitors and traders to warrant action in the case of the former, if the only objection in the case of the latter is the difficulty of proceeding; but if the Solicitor-General's major premises be granted, then it is difficult to resist his conclusion.

The opponents of the suggestion of Sir Henry Peek would *à fortiori* oppose the conclusion reached in this essay. Their reasoning when it ceases to be a variation on the argument of the Solicitor-General, is not remarkable for strength. The *Solicitors' Journal* at first adopted the pleasant vein: "We would suggest that the *Law List* should be extended so as to include a short certificate by the butcher, baker, and grocer of each solicitor, stating whether he has paid his bills with punctuality and regularity; and the name of his banker might also be given," of whom detailed particulars might be had "as to his solvency." It is sufficient to remark that insolvency, unlike a man's relations with his butcher, is a public fact; and there is no *à priori* reason why the mode of publication should be chosen with exclusive regard to the convenience of the insolvent, any more than that the course should be followed of more completely consulting his convenience by never publishing the fact at all.

The following is offered by a correspondent "S.S.C." of the *Solicitors' Journal*, 30th March, 1878, as a demonstration that, as a measure of precaution, Sir Henry Peek's proposal would be "ineffective." "In large communities the client is, as a rule, introduced to the solicitor by a common acquaintance in cases where he does not already know him personally. Whatever underhand 'touting' may go on, canvassing and advertising are not recognized with us as legitimate modes of increasing a connection. In country districts, on the other hand, a man's antecedents are pretty well known, if he has any, and a new comer is the subject of tolerably free criticism and inquiry on the part of those with whom he proposes to compete." What this passage goes to show is that the precaution is unnecessary, which is a different thing from what the writer sets out to prove. He continues still more unfortunately: "The precaution is ineffective not only on this account, but because danger to clients arises rather from the malpractice of those who have not been publicly insolvent, than from the financial weakness of those who have." By "ineffective" in this sentence is meant ineffective to guard against an evil quite foreign to the subject under discussion; it would be as rational to argue that fire insurance is an ineffective precaution against loss from fire in the case of a house liable to damage from floods.

The same writer accuses the advocates of an improved record of insolvencies of "inventing a peculiar, public and indelible disgrace." Now the first of these three adjectives can be got rid of by improving the record, as far as practicable, all round. The second and third are inapplicable: bankruptcy is already a public disgrace, and it is not an indelible disgrace—it is always open to the bankrupt to pay his former debts, and thus in the most effectual manner clear his character. This proceeding is nowadays somewhat old-fashioned and out of date, but it would be no public evil to strengthen the motives for bringing it into vogue again.

Every one acquainted with the state of public feeling must be aware that the arguments for a general improvement of the bankruptcy record have little chance of acceptance, whether this reasoning be valid or not. It is necessary, therefore, to inquire into the nature and locality of the resistance that would remain, supposing the logical battle were won. Bankruptcy is the result chiefly of fraud, or business ineptitude; but there is a residuum of pure misfortune that must not be lost sight of—the insolvency of solicitors, for example, sometimes arises through legal partnerships where the innocent practitioner is dragged down by the guilty. The resistance referred to, however, is by and on behalf of fraud. It exists in the shape of prejudice on the part of the honest: on the part of the dishonest it may be described as unhealthy moral feeling. Under the first head we may notice several plausible grounds for taking a lenient view of the matter as affecting the interests of the professional person. The first of these is the ordinary presumption in favour of what is, and what has been, against any kind of innovation. In the present case it is unnecessary to combat this presumption, it is easier to show that it does not apply. The conditions under which all professions are now exercised, have been so radically altered by the comparatively recent development of the facilities of locomotion, that certain compensatory changes are required to preserve the former balance, and to relieve honesty from the accidental disadvantage under which the old struggle with dishonesty is now maintained. It is this unobserved change, and not the necessary compensatory measures, which constitute the real innovation. In former times few people were compelled to deal with persons of whose antecedents they were ignorant. Dealings with vagabond tinkers, and with the retailers at country fairs frequently turned out disappointing, but these transactions were few in number and trifling in amount. Now this kind of risk has invaded the most serious kinds of business. Bankers of good position help to float Honduras loans, just as the retailer at the fair sold wooden nutmegs. Solicitors, on the other hand, occasionally swindle in a more direct fashion, imitating the pattern of conduct set by the tinker who decamped with the kettle he had undertaken to mend for the owner. In the most important matters we are now compelled to deal with persons essentially of the vagabond type, *i.e.*, persons about whom no information of a trustworthy kind is readily obtainable. Such persons may be honest, and generally are so, but the serious thing is that an altogether new kind of impunity is conferred upon the opposite line of conduct.

Another prejudice against any increased severity towards defaulters arises from the very general confusion of thought that prevails concerning economical phenomena. When a professional man takes a fee, or a tradesman effects a sale, the whole advantage to the community that arises out of the transaction is supposed to reside in the transfer of money from the buyer to the seller. The advantage common to the buyer and the community in the goods transferred, or the service rendered, is wholly lost sight of. Persons familiar with the free trade controversy are aware how common and deep-seated this transparent error is. The tendency of this popular error in this question is to throw a shield of a certain bastard kind of sympathy over the trader or professional man who mixes a little fraud with his business operations. A severe view of the matter appears to such persons to be in some degree dangerous to commercial prosperity. They forget two things; firstly, every illicit gain is the transfer of property from a person, probably honest, to a person who is certainly dishonest, and does not increase the sum of wealth in the community in the least; and secondly, if the fraudulent person's reputation were really known, although he would not be employed, business would not necessarily suffer, because a more honest person would probably be found to fill his place.

Another plausible reason against severity is the fact that any steps taken in the matter would have to be taken against certain definite persons, while the protection that would thereby be afforded, would be to persons of undetermined identity. It is evident that, by a well-known law of association, sympathy would be apt to take a mischievous direction in any case of this kind. To this may be added the fear that if a register of public facts as to reputations were readily accessible, the effects on some individuals would be crushing : their professional career might be altogether closed. Hence, just as juries refuse to find obviously proper verdicts, when the punishment for the offence alleged appears excessive, so people shrink from taking a measure of severity which leaves no power of mitigating the consequences to certain individuals. It is true that heavy and unexpected punishment would fall upon some persons who conduct their business upon lax principles if a new and sudden light were thrown upon their practices. But this would only happen at the commencement of the new mode of proceeding; after the change the present temptation to fraud or carelessness would be in a great measure removed, to the no small advantage of the public.

In the case of fraud it often happens that the honest part of the transaction confers more advantage on the person defrauded than the loss occasioned by the fraud, so that, after reckoning fraud, a balance of gain remains to the person defrauded. This helps to explain the comparative lenity with which fraud is treated. The fraud does not cease to be destructive to industry and the general wealth of the community when its amount is small compared with the total transactions. It then resembles the petty larcenies to which some kinds of business are constantly liable.

The unhealthy moral feeling that impedes right thinking on this subject is found in the general laxity of judgment with regard to fraud. Some insolvents are perfectly innocent in their inability to meet their engagements, and it may be thought that the indisposition to anything like stringent treatment arises solely from the fear of injuring the innocent as well as the guilty. A knowledge of contemporary social facts will dispel this illusion. It is admitted in the abstract that fraud ought to be punished, but the mildest actual proposals to punish will be found by wide commercial circles needlessly severe. The facts under this head have been brought into unpleasant prominence of late in public discussion and by Parliamentary investigation. Financial operations on a large scale have been unmasked, and have been shown to have been unadulterated fraud from the beginning. Recent correspondence in the *Times* has shown that commerce is honeycombed with the system of commissions, *i.e.*, bribes to agents to betray trust. The process of fraud, or the flaunting of the proceeds of fraud, meets one on every hand. A living novelist makes one of his characters say: "It is in everybody's mouth that successful swindlers may buy up half the land in the country." A more unpleasant fact is that with the land social position is purchased also, unless the swindling is of an obtrusively disagreeable kind.

The failure of one notorious person to purchase social position with the proceeds of gigantic frauds, has recently drawn a good deal of attention. It is certainly to the credit of society that he did fail, but the episode, nevertheless, furnishes this damaging evidence; the person in question is not deficient in tact and intelligence, and he must have formed a low estimate of English society before he made the attempt. The attempt moreover partially succeeded, and was in a great measure foiled by the relentless persecution of one enemy, a gentleman to whom that part of the English public, which is not desirous that successful fraud shall remain a recognized mode of social promotion, is much indebted.

One more piece of evidence may be culled from the proceedings in a comparatively recent prosecution for fraud of a most impudent type. The case is known as the Eupion case. It was an attempt to use the rules of the Stock Exchange to defraud, not the public, but the members of the Stock Exchange. This was, undoubtedly, carrying the joke too far, and the Committee of the Stock Exchange very rightly insisted on a prosecution. The piece of evidence as to the prevalence of fraud in the community was furnished by the arguments of the counsel for the defendants, and the general impression that the assertion on which its validity rested was true. He contended that although the operation attempted by his clients was undoubtedly fraudulent, it was too much in harmony with the practice and traditions of the Stock Exchange to form a proper ground for a criminal prosecution.

A curious and fatal sign of the times is that moral judgment seems meekly to wait on legal punishment, and to have no independent existence of its own. A man does not lose caste by enriching himself by fraudulent means, so long as he keeps clear of the clutches of the law; so that if rascality were strong and organised enough to take the law into its pay, as it did a few years since in New York, there would no longer be any reprobation left in any quarter. A legal decision is a useful guide to the facts of a case, but its chief significance ought to be in satisfying and giving expression to the current moral feeling. Where the moral feeling really exists, it would be intensified by any failure to reach a culprit in consequence of defects in legal machinery.

The different measures which are meted to fraud and theft have no justification, although the fact of the difference is of capital importance as an evidence of social feeling. Fraud and theft are precisely similar in their effect on the general wealth; except that fraud has frequently indirect damaging effects of much greater consequence than the direct loss: the difference is one of accident only. Fraud may be defined as diluted theft. The fraudulent person differs from the common robber in combining the fraud with an operation of a legitimate commercial character, and consequently obtaining the consent of the victim to the whole transaction.

A farmer for example may buy six bags of genuine seed. On his way home one of them may be stolen, and, for the sake of the parallelism, let us suppose the seller of the seed to be the thief. He may at another time buy what he supposes to be six bags of genuine seed, but one-sixth of the whole may by the fraud of the second seller be "killed" seed. Now the injury to the farmer in the case of the theft is much less than in the case of the fraud, because he is not subjected to the further loss that the fraud occasions, of miscalculation in sowing his land. The thievish seller, however, would be liable to a swift and almost savage punishment, and would be socially ruined; while the fraudulent seller, until quite recently, might carry on such operations with perfect impunity. And even now that the law has been changed in a fragmentary way to meet this special case, the punishment legally and socially is not a tithe of that meted to the thief.

The popular judgment with respect to fraud is based to a considerable extent on the opinions of the large number of persons who deprecate the application of first principles to the criticism of commercial transactions for reasons not entirely speculative. Some of these are intellectually unable to draw the fine distinctions between "*meum*" and "*tuum*" required by perfect honesty in complex pecuniary transactions; and consequently enjoy the double advantage of keeping up a kind of conscience, and at the same time, by deciding all doubtful points of honesty in their own favour, contrive to get a good share of the illicit gains so plentiful in the commercial world. Another class rely upon no intellectual difficulties, but resolutely act upon a liberal interpretation of the convenient motto "business is business."

If the disposition to treat fraud with due severity could be induced, the case of business ineptitude would not present much difficulty. The remedy of publicity would be found efficacious for both, without being so unjust to the latter as at first appears; for the sting of publicity resides in the disagreeable character of the facts exposed. It is evident that the foolish person, who involves other people in loss, is a commercial danger of a similar kind to the fraudulent person, and it is right that people who encounter the risk of dealing with him should do it with their eyes open.

There remains the case of pure misfortune, which is neither fraud nor folly. This is a difficulty, but the proposition to meet it by leaving the whole business in general confusion, is quite inadmissible. The best solution would be to make the record as full as possible, so as to allow of qualification of the bare fact of insolvency by persons and societies of influence. The Council of the Incorporated Law Society could, for example, as already explained, protect the interests of innocently insolvent solicitors.

Should it be conceded that the natural and just remedy for the evil of reckless and fraudulent insolvency is the provision by authority of a "proper record," there would still remain the important question of opportuneness, which chiefly turns upon the public disposition with regard to fraud. Stringent laws against theft are of no avail until the bulk of the community forswears the practice of thieving; nor would it be possible in a free community to get such laws passed with a view to *bond fide* administration. The attempt would only fritter the moral force that might easily be directed to more hopeful and fruitful uses. In the progress of society, a compact body of public opinion is much sooner available against the practice of thieving than against its more complex, but equally immoral congener, that of cheating. Therefore it is of no advantage to press even a wise and righteous measure for immediate adoption if the resistance offered by stupidity and sinister interest is of too serious a character. The first thing is to enlighten a sufficient number of people to give the necessary weight of numbers to move with effect. It is probable that if a decision were hastily made to adopt Sir Henry Peek's proposal, a general opinion would prevail that a step of unnecessary harshness had been taken; the decision might be reversed, and the ultimate triumph of a sound policy would be retarded instead of being hastened.

The essential thing is to show a steady front to public opinion, to brand fraud with its proper name, no matter how many and how influential are the people who practise it and connive at it, and at the same time not to flinch from urging the hearty acceptance of the proper remedy for fraud, namely, as perfect publicity as possible. This publicity, owing to the changed circumstances of the time, cannot now be obtained without common action, and people have not yet comprehended the necessities of the new situation. Fraud should be met and defeated by the public authority with as much care and determination as theft.

The task is, in fact, simpler and easier ; for in the case of theft, it is necessary to detect and seize the wrongdoer, in the case of fraud all that is necessary is to give the intended victim the means of ascertaining the character of the intending cheat. Combined action against theft is a necessity from the very beginning of society; on the other hand, it only begins to be necessary against fraud when common report, owing to the complexity and size of modern societies, ceases to give the requisite warning against rogues.

The question of defaulting lawyers is not likely to be dealt with successfully if a sectional remedy only is sought ; but treated as part of a wider question, it offers a good opportunity in the first place for the advocacy, and in the second for the application of the first instalment of a general method of treatment for the prevalent commercial fraud and the recklessness that can with difficulty be distinguished from it. The insolvency of solicitors is admittedly less excusable than that of traders, and also a complete register exists in the *Law List*—two facts which afford excellent reasons for selecting insolvent solicitors as the object of the first attack. Undertaken from this point of view, the addition to the *Law List* in the case of solicitors once, twice, or more times bankrupt, of the dates of bankruptcy, dividends paid, and references to detailed information would have a great and wholesome effect, and would powerfully help to put the public on the right track for dealing with the general evil of fraud, which has become a social scandal and a grave danger for the future of British commerce.

CERTIFICATE OF MERIT.

MR. JAMES WHITE.

On the 29th January, 1878, Sir Henry Peek asked the following question of the Solicitor-General:—" Whether he has considered the desirability (in addition to the other information contained in the annual *Law List*, published by authority) of, in the case of solicitors once, twice, or more times bankrupt, giving the dates of bankruptcy, dividends paid, and the names of assignees of whom detailed particulars might be had; also, in the case of solicitors whose names do not continuously appear in the *Law List*, the reason for omission in occasional years being explained."

This question was noticed, and commented upon, in a somewhat flippant article in the *Solicitors' Journal*. The article elicited a letter from Sir Henry Peek, in which he quoted a letter he had received from Mr. Munton, solicitor, as a justification of his question.

A correspondence of considerable length, in which Sir Henry Peek, Mr. Munton, and a writer under the *nom de plume* of " S.S.C." bore the principal part, ensued. This correspondence was, as to the bulk of it, published in the *Solicitors' Journal*, which paper also published some articles upon the subject.

To a consideration of the "points and remedies" adverted to in the correspondence and articles referred to, the following remarks are addressed.

In the correspondence the following evils, said to be prevalent in the solicitor's profession, are pointed out and commented on, viz.:—

(1.) The insolvency of solicitors. This is the principal evil to which Sir Henry Peek addresses himself.

(2.) "The unaccountably long time large sums are frequently held by solicitors as assignees or acting for assignees of insolvent estates."

(3.) That certain practitioners purposely take out their certificates too late for their names to be inserted in the *Law List* for the ensuing year.

(4.) General malpractices of the profession. I shall define what I wish to indicate by this head presently.

It will be convenient to deal with these points separately and in order, and first let us take "Insolvency."

This is the point, as I have before remarked, to which Sir Henry Peek principally addresses himself, and is the evil which more particularly prompted his question. That question would seem to have been asked before Sir Henry Peek had armed himself with any precise statistics, and to have been suggested by his general opinions merely.

Later on in the correspondence Mr. Munton comes to his support with figures of great value, and with assertions which excited surprise---nay, almost ridicule—in the writer of the articles in the *Solicitors' Journal*. Still later Sir Henry Peek obtained statistics checking and corroborating one of Mr. Munton's assertions.

Mr. Munton's assertions and statistics may be usefully extracted from the correspondence. In a letter to *The Echo* newspaper of February 15th, 1878, Mr. Munton says:—"At an early period after the 1861 Act came into operation, I was so much struck with the frequency of solicitors passing through the Court, that I commenced making a regular note of them in my *Law List*; and some years back I publicly drew the attention of the Incorporated Law Society (in a speech which was reported in most journals at the time) to the astonishing fact that scarcely a single page of the book was without one or more marks of reference. But more recently, the number of bankruptcies, liquidations, or compositions by professional men has increased at a greater rate still; and at this date my notes in question present a most formidable appearance. I am almost tempted to give the exact figures, but perhaps I have said enough for the purpose. Those who have had any experience in the matter know that professional men rarely become bankrupt incidental to their true calling, and it is easy to understand why this is so, for the very nature of the solicitor's avocation—and, *à fortiori*, the barrister's—excludes him from such losses as commonly belong to commerce.

"It is the desire of people to dabble in matters altogether

foreign to their occupation, which leads to monetary ruin; and I, for one, should not be sorry to see ample publicity given to all failures traceable to speculation. These occurrences are very detrimental to the legal profession at large, for such things give rise to a widespread distrust, whereby the innocent are made to suffer with the guilty."

These statements having been questioned by the *Solicitors' Journal*, a discussion ensued which resulted in Sir Henry Peek writing to that paper, "that he had had the antecedents of 155 London solicitors under the letter D, in the present *Law List*, taken out, with the result that eleven names (or seven per cent.) were before him as having, some once, some twice, more or less discreditably figured in the *Gazette*—proving conclusively that the ventilation of the subject would be neither time nor trouble thrown away."

Finally Mr. Munton gave the following figures, in reply to an article in the *Solicitors' Journal*. The number of solicitors who failed in practice in the years undermentioned were as follows:—

Year.	No. of Failures.	Year.	No. of Failures.	Year.	No. of Failures.
1862	83	1867	101	1872	21
1863	60	1868	93	1873	25
1864	61	1869	94	1874	31
1865	59	1870	16	1875	34
1866	65	1871	29	1876	38

These figures were not in the correspondence either impugned or corroborated.

Mr. Munton further calculated roughly that at least one solicitor in every twenty (or five per cent.) becomes bankrupt. The foregoing, I think, comprises in substance the statements made and statistics adduced in the correspondence, relative to point No. 1.

Before discussing them, I shall extract the statements made in regard to the other points from the correspondence.

With respect to the point which I have numbered (2.), viz:— that referred to by Sir Henry Peek in the following words, "the unaccountably long time large sums are frequently held by solicitors as assignees or acting for assignees of insolvent estates." This is adverted to by Sir Henry Peek alone. No facts respecting it were stated in the correspondence, and it does not seem to have been considered of much importance. I think I may also safely dismiss it from consideration, and for the following reasons:—In the first place, solicitors seldom act as assignees. In fact, this is one of the grievances of the profession, or at any rate of a part of it. Again, if, when acting for assignees, they retain money as alleged, that, surely, is through the negligence of the assignees. Further, supposing such misdoings to be prevalent, the existing law of bankruptcy provides a sufficient remedy.

To pass on now to our third point, "that certain practitioners purposely take out their certificates too late for their names to be inserted in the *Law List* for the ensuing year." It is well known in the profession that unless a solicitor takes out his certificate before the 1st January in each year, his name does not appear in the *Law List* for that year. Mr. Munton, Sir Henry Peek, and the *Solicitors' Journal* are under the impression that there are certain discreditable members of the profession, who, by taking out their certificates after the 1st January, purposely avoid appearing in the *Law List*. The *Solicitors' Journal*, in exculpation of the profession, takes the trouble to give figures (under 100) showing the small number of certificates so taken out per annum. I venture to think, however, that there are very few (if any) solicitors who intentionally take out their certificates too late. In fact, as "S.S.C.," in one of his very thoughtful and temperate letters has pointed out the omission of the name from the *Law List*, would be so suggestive of suspicion that the man of defaulting proclivities would be careful to have his name figuring in the list, and only carelessness or extreme impecuniosity could lead to such omission. There are many reasons other than intentional neglect why many solicitors' names do not appear in the list for the current year. In the first place there are, no doubt, many omissions through carelessness or accident. Again, amongst the certificates taken out after the 1st January would be those of solicitors admitted after that date. From experience, however, I incline to think, that amongst the discreditable class of solicitors at any rate, the omission to take out a certificate in time is the result of "extreme impecuniosity." To have his name omitted from the *Law List* is itself a source of inconvenience and annoyance to a solicitor. The *Law List* is evidence of the fact that he is a solicitor, and that he has taken out a certificate for the current year, and he would have, were his name omitted from the list, to procure other evidence should the fact be questioned. Besides this, every solicitor who deals with another, a stranger to him, almost mechanically looks at his list to see who and what the stranger is, and if his name were not in the list, would probably make inquiries before transacting business with him.

There does not, therefore, seem to me to be in this point any evil which requires a remedy, and I shall not further consider it.

I shall turn next to point "No. (4:)"—"General Malpractices" I have termed it. Sir Henry Peek, when he asked his question in the House, does not seem to have had this point in mind. In fact it seems to have been suggested by the correspondent, whom I might but for the almost judicial character of his letters, term one of Sir Henry's opponents. "S.S.C." in a letter of April 6th, 1878, to the Editor of the *Solicitors' Journal*, writes:—"Every case of reckless insolvency might, I fear, be capped by one of malpractice deserving public reprimand, if not punishment. There are solicitors who habitually shuffle off the settlement of undisputed claims to the very verge of extreme proceedings. There are those whose course of practice is a standing discredit to their profession, and a continual nuisance to their professional brethren." Here I should premise what I wish to indicate by the term "general malpractice." I wish to indicate not such misconduct as would bring the practitioner as a member of the community at large within the pale of the law, nor such professional misconduct as a solicitor as is punishable by striking him off the rolls. This last I shall touch upon later on. But I wish to indicate those acts or omissions which are marked by the terms "dishonorable," "discreditable," "sharp practice," &c., when viewed from a high professional point of view. I presume this is the meaning intended by "S.S.C." in the extract from his letter above quoted.

Here then we have, I think, an evil worthy of discussion and consideration.

Two out of our four points have been disposed of. The remaining two, however, "Insolvency" and "General Malpractice" afford ample food for reflection.

And first I shall deal with insolvency. In so doing I shall find it necessary to make a few preliminary remarks as to the statistics furnished by Mr. Munton and Sir Henry Peek.

With respect to the statement of the latter that "eleven out of 155 solicitors under the letter "D" have more or less discreditably figured in the *Gazette*, I may remark that in my opinion the doubt attempted to be thrown upon it by the *Solicitors' Journal* is quite without foundation. To say that a mistake may have been made is to say only what may truthfully be said of all human acts—of course, a mistake may have been made. The method adopted by Sir Henry Peek is, however, the most sure known to me. The trade registries have very complete and conveniently arranged registers, and their searches are made by clerks whose constant practice renders them almost infallible.

Now as to Mr. Munton's figures. It is almost impossible for any one to check these unless he possesses a noted-up *Law List* similar to that referred to by Mr. Munton, or unless as Sir Henry Peek checked them, which would only be done at considerable expense. I have, however, made some effort to ascertain if Mr. Munton's figures were at any rate approximately correct, by searching the ordinary weekly register supplied by one of the leading trade protection societies for two years, which I selected haphazard. I have taken out with so much accuracy as I could command, the figures for the years 1874 and 1876. As it was but little extra trouble I divided the failures into liquidations and bankruptcies, and for the purposes of comparison I made similar searches against auctioneers and accountants during the same years. A comparison of the following table with Mr. Munton's figures at p. 97 will show how far my figures agree with his.

FAILURES IN THE YEAR 1874.

	Accountants.	Auctioneers.	Solicitors.
Liquidations	17	41	16
Bankruptcies	19	27	14
Total of Failures	36	68	30

FAILURES IN THE YEAR 1876.

	Accountants.	Auctioneers.	Solicitors.
Liquidations	9	42	14
Bankruptcies	15	30	17
Total of Failures	24	72	31

It will be seen that my figures do not quite tally with Mr. Munton's. The differences, however, are not so great as to be of much importance. My examination of the registers would seem to show, as will appear from my table, that there is no ground for the statement that the bulk of solicitors' failures is on their own petition. Leaving the statistics, let me consider some of Mr. Munton's assertions in his published letters. He says, "Few lawyers have honestly occasion to fail," and again, "professional men rarely become bankrupt incidental to their true calling, and it is easy to understand, &c." Now to these assertions, I am with the utmost deference compelled to take exception. "S.S.C." has already pointed out "that confidence is not all on one side, and that it is no unheard of thing for solicitors to incur very heavy losses, not only of costs, but of cash, by mistaken confidence in the integrity or discretion of their clients." And this confidence is, I believe, a fruitful source of insolvency to solicitors. Then, again, many an honest man and good lawyer is compelled to start in practice with an insufficient capital and less sufficient connection. Here is a case, and one of frequent occurrence, where a failure may be perfectly "honest," and "incidental to the true calling" of a solicitor. In fact, many cases could be pointed out in which solicitors do and can "honestly" fail, but I content myself with calling attention to two of (perhaps) the most frequent occurrence. Again Mr. Munton would "like to have ample publicity given to failures traceable to speculation." Surely Mr. Munton would never contend that a solicitor may not invest any spare capital or income he may be possessed of, in a fair and reasonable speculation which afforded a probable prospect of success. How many, I wonder, of the numerous practitioners who have retired from business with a competency have so retired on the profits resulting from their profession alone? The "speculation" part of the question would be met, I suppose, by the classification of failures which Mr. Munton assumes into "honest" and "dishonest." Such a classification can, it is evident, only be made by a comparison with some standard, or by reference to some definition. What this standard or definition should be I shall discuss later on, and there I shall inferentially deal with the "speculation" evil.

There is, however, an all-important question, which lies on the threshold of our inquiry. Why should solicitors be subjected to exceptional legislation in respect of their failures or malpractices? Are any exceptional privileges conferred upon them by the law as a compensation? I am aware of none. The privileges conferred on solicitors are conferred rather for the benefit of the community than for the benefit of the profession. However, Mr. Munton has suggested an answer to our question. He says, solicitors are "pre-eminently trusted." Now, I fail to see that in a monetary way (in respect of which only could insolvency at any rate prejudice the trust reposed) solicitors are pre-eminently trusted. In fact, from the monetary point of view, I think a little reflection will show that a solicitor is as little trusted, or less trusted, than most other classes. I feel that this statement will seem at first sight rather startling, but I am convinced of its truth.

The trust reposed in a solicitor, of which we hear and say so much, is not a trust of money or valuable securities, but rather the confidence with which a client entrusts his solicitor with the arrangement and settlement of important affairs—the confidence with which he leaves him unfettered to deal as he in his discretion thinks best for his client's interest, in cases in which such interest often involves his client's reputation, solvency, or even his domestic happiness. This is, I take it, what a man means when he says to his solicitor:—"I repose the utmost trust and confidence in you; I have given you information which, if improperly disclosed, might lead to my ruin." But how does a solicitor's insolvency necessarily affect this confidence? Does a solicitor the moment he becomes insolvent become dishonorable? Surely not. Now compare for a moment the amounts and securities entrusted to the hands of solicitors with those deposited with private banking firms, with the credit given in the everyday dealings of commerce by one merchant to another, often without the slightest security; follow out the comparison through all classes to its fullest extent, and the result I have stated above, viz., that solicitors are not, from a monetary point of view, pre-eminently trusted, must, it seems to me, follow upon such comparison.

Again I see that Mr. Munton has, in a recent letter to the *Law Times*, stated that "many people, especially the uneducated, trust a solicitor simply because he is a solicitor." Such a statement as this can only be based upon experience. I think, however, that there are many solicitors could be found who devoutly wish this statement were true. The suspicion and distrust with which the uneducated regard and have, since time was, regarded lawyers, is sufficiently exemplified in the "proverbial philosophy" of all countries.

As I have said before, insolvency pure and simple, by which I mean insolvency not dishonest, need not in any way prevent a solicitor from honorably and efficiently carrying on his practice. Many solicitors, it is true, have grafted on to the ordinary duties of their profession the business of estate agents and financiers, and, as to such, it is apparent that their insolvency would interfere with the proper discharge of the duties they had assumed.

Further, as the *Solicitors' Journal* has pointed out, in the country at all events, a solicitor's antecedents are perfectly well known; and even in London it is not the habit of clients to turn for advice into the first solicitor's office they pass. Besides this, the public have the same notice of the insolvency of solicitors through the medium of the trade and other journals as they have of the insolvency of all other classes.

The statement that the insolvencies of solicitors are very detrimental to the legal profession at large, and give rise to widespread distrust, I venture to doubt. The whole question must turn on the fact, whether an average failure of thirty-five per annum in the solicitor's profession is a larger average than that which obtains in other professions or callings. This has not been shown, and from the figures I have taken out, showing the number of failures of auctioneers and accountants, I should much doubt if it be the fact. It is impossible for me to compare exactly the failures of solicitors with those of accountants and auctioneers, as I cannot ascertain with precision the aggregate of the two latter classes. The result of inquiries I have made would lead me to believe that solicitors are about seven times more numerous than accountants, about six times more numerous than auctioneers.

In London there are, roughly speaking, about 660 accountants, and 736 auctioneers, and from an inspection of the country directories, I gather that these proportions are fairly maintained throughout the country. If these figures are correct, they would show that, as compared with auctioneers and accountants, solicitors are an exceptionally solvent class. For, although on the aggregate six times more numerous than auctioneers, their annual average of failures would be about half those of auctioneers. In other words, the failures of auctioneers are twelve times more numerous than those of solicitors, and, working out the comparison between solicitors and accountants in the same way, it would seem that the failures of accountants are in proportion about six times more numerous than those of solicitors. If then the percentage of insolvents amongst solicitors be not abnormally large, why should the outside public look upon the profession as a body with widespread distrust?

I think, then, that it cannot be shown that exceptional legislation is required for the protection of the outside public, either on the ground that solicitors are pre-eminently trusted, or that the percentage of failures amongst them is abnormally large.

Now let us turn to what I have termed "General Malpractice." Here again, so far as regards the outside public, I am bound to come to the same conclusion as I do with respect to professional insolvency, and for similar reasons, viz.:—(1.) That the privileges enjoyed by solicitors are not so great, nor the position allotted to them by the law, and by public estimation so high, that the outside public have a right to expect from them exceptional fair dealing, and (2.) The malpractices of solicitors are not more numerous in proportion, so far as I am aware, than those of any other profession or calling.

Let us now regard the question from a professional point of view. The reputation, nay, the very existence of a profession, depends on its members fixing for themselves, a high standard of morality and honour, and steadfastly adhering to it.

It needs must be a higher one than that conformed to by the masses. As "S.S.C." has written, "the rules of conduct which should guide the solicitor, are more strict than those which suffice for the ways of commerce, he must frequently deny himself gains, which on commercial principles he might legitimately secure, there is scarcely any calling in which honesty (in its truest sense) is so often not the best policy for the pocket."

Taking the high standard to which it should be the aim of a profession, worthy of the name, to conform, having regard to the fact, that solicitors are officers of our Courts of Justice, it must be acknowledged, that the evils which I have termed insolvency and general malpractice, exist, and require a remedy.

There is a well-known process of punishment for solicitors who are guilty of certain offences. That is, striking them off the roll of solicitors. This punishment deprives them of the position, which they have to spend, as a rule, large sums of money, and five of the best years of their lives, to attain; deprives them, in fact, in most cases, of the means of earning a livelihood.

This it will be readily conceived, is not a punishment to be inflicted on slight provocation, and yet it is sometimes suffered for an offence which might be termed "malpractice." But the malpractice for which it is suffered, is malpractice in the capacity of officer of the Court, not as a member of a profession setting a high standard of morality for its members to conform to. A solicitor may be struck off the rolls, when he is convicted of an indictable offence, or circumstances amounting to an indictable offence are admitted by or proved against him; for acting for an unqualified person, or for professional misconduct. It will be found that all the cases coming under the head of professional misconduct, are cases more immediately connected with the solicitor's duties as an officer of the Court.

A solicitor has a threefold character with rights and duties divers, though not diverse, grouped about each. His character as an officer of the Court—his character as a member of an honorable profession—and his character as a member of the community at large.

Now, neither insolvency, nor what I have termed general malpractice are punishable by striking off the roll. Insolvency indeed, is punishable where there is a clear case of fraudulent appropriation of client's moneys, which ought to have been paid over. But insolvency not so punishable, and malpractice, are matters which it seems to me affect the character of a solicitor as a member of a profession, not as an officer of the Court, not as a member of the community at large. They must be remedied in order to preserve that high professional feeling which I have before referred to.

Now, what is to be the nature of the remedy.

Sir Henry Peek suggested marking the names of the offending parties in the *Law List*, but this suggestion he has since abandoned, and it seems impossible to support it.

As "S.S.C." has remarked, "the only fitting mode of dealing with the matter is one of discipline," and he thinks that "the proper dispenser of that discipline is the Incorporated Law Society in its capacity of registry of solicitors." Such discipline, he says, "should not be inquisitorial; but an overt act, such as bankruptcy, should form the subject of inquiry, and a List of publicly insolvent Solicitors should be compiled, and available for reference.

"Such a list should distinguish those cases, in which a fair inquiry had shown that failure did not result from speculation, extravagance, or neglect.

"In these inquiries, the councils of local law societies should co-operate. I do not think they should decide because the sectarian animosities in politics and religion which become so personal in all but the largest communities, would often colourably, if not fairly, be asserted to have influenced their verdict.

"The proposed list of names might not improperly be appended to the annual report, and the honorable, but unfortunate, man would be rather benefited than injured by such publication."

I have quoted "S.S.C." at length on this point, both because he and Mr. Munton agree on it, and because I am entirely of the same opinion.

The proposition is, "the matter is one of professional discipline, and the proper dispenser of that discipline is the Incorporated Law Society." Now, as to the working out of the details of this proposition, there seems to be a slight difference of opinion between "S.S.C." and Mr. Munton.

The latter proposed, "to move at the next annual meeting of the Incorporated Law Society for the appointment of a vigilance committee, to be charged with the special duty of inquiring into malpractices and defalcations, and as to bankruptcy, I propose that in the absence of reasonable explanation (*i.e.*, it should be incumbent on a bankrupt solicitor, having regard to his position of trust, to establish a *primâ facie* misfortune), the council should be empowered to oppose the renewal of certificates."

"S.S.C." objected that—

(1). "A self-constituted vigilance committee is abnormal in its nature, and very liable to be fitful and uneven in its action: what we need is a recognised authority, acting regularly and dispassionately—a public prosecutor in fact."

(2.) "To prevent the renewal of a solicitor's certificate,

comes practically to the same thing as striking him off the roll, and that extreme penalty would not be properly applicable to many cases which would deserve the pillory."

Mr. Munton then explained the nature of his vigilance committee. It was to consist of twelve members, half to be selected from the council of the Society, half from "undoubtedly respectable ordinary members." The president of the council should be chairman, and the registrar should attend *ex officio*.

This sub-committee should report to the general body of the council as such, and it would be for them to take action on the result.

Mr. Munton subsequently stated that the question of the penalty to be inflicted required consideration.

Here I have at last come to entirely new ground—no details as to the penalties have been worked out either in the correspondence or articles, save those above suggested by Mr. Munton.

Mr. Munton's proposal would not, I think, work. I do not believe that any vigilance committee could be found who would undertake the necessary inquiries. They would occupy too much time.

Such inquiries could not, I think, be undertaken by any one committee. I am aware that the committee of the London Stock Exchange perform similar duties to those proposed for Mr. Munton's vigilance committee; but then the number of their members is small and compact.

Take the failures only. As Mr. Munton's table shows, the number of failures averages about thirty-five per annum. Now the work of the inquiries into these thirty-five failures would not be light. Add to these the numerous inquiries into malpractices, which the knowledge that an expeditious mode of punishing the offenders was ready to hand, would induce, and I think the committee would have so much work that even Mr. Munton, enthusiastic as he is for professional reform, would not care to be a member. It is almost certain that the inquiries into malpractices would at first be very numerous, although it is to be hoped that they would gradually diminish.

The proposal of "S.S.C." that the local societies should assist in the inquiries, struck me at first sight as valuable, but the very objection which he raises to their deciding a case, applies with equal force to their making inquiries. We have all heard of one-sided inquiries. There are, however, more cogent reasons than this, viz., that the local law societies are not sufficiently numerous, they are many of them of indifferent repute in their localities, most of them are very poorly supported and patronised by the profession. They are not sufficiently official. I assent entirely to the proposition that the Incorporated Law Society should be the dispenser of discipline, but I do not think the local law societies are desirable agents.

It seems to me that a committee of any sort is eminently ill qualified to undertake inquiries. There should be a paid officer appointed for the purpose. I shall consider as to how this and any other suggestions I make, are to be carried into effect later on.

The officer appointed should have power to compel the production of witnesses and documents, and of receiving evidence on oath, and any other auxiliary powers necessary for making a complete inquiry. He should then furnish a report to the council of the society, who should consider and decide upon it.

So much for the method of inquiry. Now let us consider what inquiries should be made. In the case of insolvencies, I think the inquiries made should be such as would elicit such facts as would enable the council to place the insolvent in one of the three following classes :—

(1.) Where the failure is honest, *i.e.*, occasioned by circumstances over which a man of ordinary prudence and foresight has no control, *e.g.*, ill-health, bad debts, loss through failure of principals, loss through a fair and legitimate and provident speculation.

(2.) Where there are no circumstances, or fraud, or improper conduct on the part of the insolvent, but where the failure is occasioned by circumstances which a man of ordinary prudence and foresight could have avoided, *e.g.*, reckless investment, improvident trust in third party, &c.

(3.) Cases in which the circumstances disclose not merely improvidence, but exhibit a dishonourable, improper, or unprofessional conduct on the part of the debtor.

As to the inquiries into the malpractices, the facts should be so stated as to enable the council to distinguish the cases into classes which I would classify as :—

(1.) Unprofessional conduct, not punishable by striking off the rolls. Such as, "touting," endeavouring to lead away a brother solicitor's clients. Treating directly with the client of a brother solicitor, in a case in which he is engaged, &c.

(2.) Disgraceful or dishonorable conduct not punishable by striking off the rolls, not as between members of the same profession merely, but as between solicitor and client—man and man—as causing the client to incur heavy and unnecessary costs, &c., refusing to satisfy an undoubtedly clear claim, &c.

I am quite conscious that the classifications I have suggested do not indicate any hard and fast line. I do not think it is possible so to do. All questions of conduct are questions of degree, and we cannot all have in our minds the same standard of excellence, but still the classes I have indicated would afford some measure of the degree of the offence.

Next let us consider what course should be adopted by the council, or, if needs be, what punishment should be inflicted.

To mark the names of offenders in the *Law List* would not, it seems to me, be of any avail. For first, the *Law List* is a book not generally referred to by persons outside the profession; and in the next place, the offenders, although pilloried in this manner, are still at liberty to practise, and would probably not be deterred from these malpractices by such a punishment.

Suspension from practice, a penalty which has on recent occasions been inflicted by the Court, seems to me the most manageable, convenient, and effective penalty. It is an effectual notice to a solicitor's clients of his misconduct, and to his fellow-professionals who are immediately connected with him. It involves sufficient pecuniary loss to make misconduct unprofitable.

It is, on the other hand, not such a punishment as entirely destroys his credit or practice. If inflicted, however, for a longer term than three years, it would probably cause a solicitor to lose his practice almost entirely; leaving him, nevertheless, at liberty to make a fresh start.

Now to turn to the application of this punishment.

In my first class of insolvents, I take it no one would contend that any punishment should be inflicted.

In my second, I should suggest on a first failure a caution merely; and on a second failure, suspension from practice for a term varying according to the circumstances of the case, but not to exceed six months.

In the third class, the punishment should, according to circumstances, be suspension for any term not exceeding three years.

In cases of unprofessional conduct, the council should, according to the circumstances, administer a private caution or public reprimand; or, if the case deserved it, give the names of the parties in their annual or other circulars, and post them in the hall of the society.

In very gross cases, the punishment of suspension for short terms might be inflicted.

As to my second class of malpractices, I think it would be found that terms of suspension varying from one to twelve months would not be too severe.

In administering these punishments, the council would, of course, be able to take into consideration all mitigating circumstances.

There should I think be an appeal from the council in cases where suspension for more than six months has been ordered, to the President of the Queen's Bench, Common Pleas, or Exchequer Divisions of the High Court of Justice, or to the Master of the Rolls.

An Act authorising the council to make rules and regulations (with the consent of the judges above-mentioned), for the discipline of solicitors in the matters referred to, and empowering the council to inflict the punishment of suspension for a term not to exceed three years (subject to the appeal referred to above), and also conferring on any officer appointed by the council to make the inquiries above suggested, the necessary powers of compelling evidence and providing that disobedience to the orders of the council should be punishable in the same manner as contempt of Court, would probably effect all that is required.

Of the fact that the powers to be conferred on the council would have to receive careful consideration, no one can be more conscious than myself. I am pleased that in an essay of this kind it is only open to me to sketch out the principal points and details of the remedies suggested; for easy as it is to suggest broad principles, it is very difficult to carry them to their fullest extent and provide the means for working them out. The means of meeting the costs occasioned by the adoption of the remedies suggested I purposely omit to discuss. This, though not a minor point, is a question to which the society would have but little difficulty in finding an answer.

That by the adoption of the remedies proposed the profession would be much benefited I confidently believe. That the public also would be benefited there can be no doubt. In reforming themselves, solicitors will benefit the community at large. They need not have the benefit of that community directly in view, for in seeking the advancement and purification of their profession in a fair and legitimate manner, they must needs incite other professions and callings to look to themselves. That the outside public is now turning its attention to the reform of the solicitor's profession, does not indicate that that profession is becoming worse, but simply that the public looks for a higher standard of morality. Better far will it be for the profession if it reforms itself than that the hand of the legislature set in motion by outsiders should reform it. Solicitors are not exceptional in being threatened with legislative interference. We have already had a Stock Exchange Commission, and accountants of questionable reputation are beginning to quake at the prospect of a remodelling of the Bankruptcy Laws.

Let the profession then look to itself. It should not regard Sir Henry Peek in the light of an enemy, but rather as a friend giving the warning, "Be wise in time." Having reformed itself, it can then turn round and endeavour to get the legislature to remedy the many grievances under which it labours; it may fairly ask that solicitor's offices shall not be given to barristers, and that unauthorised persons should be restrained from practising a profession for which they have not qualified, and that professional fees may be increased in proportion with the decrease which the value of money has sustained since those fees first were fixed.

www.ingramcontent.com/pod-product-compliance
Lightning Source LLC
Chambersburg PA
CBHW022133160426
43197CB00009B/1269